PrincetonReview.com

GUIDING TEENS

WITH LEARNING

DISABILITIES

NAVIGATING THE TRANSITION FROM
HIGH SCHOOL TO ADULTHOOD

Arlyn Roffman, PhD

Featuring a chapter by
Loring C. Brinckerhoff, PhD

Random House, Inc.
New York

The Princeton Review, Inc.
2315 Broadway
New York, NY 10024
E-mail: bookeditor@review.com

ISBN 978-0-375-76496-7

Publisher: Robert Franek
Senior Editor: Adrinda Kelly
Editor: Suzanne J. Podhurst
Designer and Production Manager: Scott Harris
Production Editor: Christine LaRubio

Printed in the United States of America.

9 8 7 6 5 4 3 2 1

2008 Edition

ABOUT THE AUTHOR

Arlyn Roffman, PhD, is a licensed psychologist and a full-time professor at Lesley University, where she served as the founding director of Threshold, a transition program for young adults with learning disabilities (LD). Dr. Roffman has served on the professional advisory boards of several national organizations related to LD and has consulted and made conference presentations on issues related to special education and psychology throughout the U.S. and abroad. She is the author of numerous books, articles, and chapters on LD-related challenges. Dr. Roffman, her husband, and daughter live in the Boston area. She can be reached at ARoffman@lesley.edu.

ABOUT THE CONTRIBUTING AUTHOR

Loring C. Brinckerhoff, PhD, is Director of the Office of Disability Policy at Educational Testing Service (ETS). He also serves as a higher education and disability consultant to Recording for the Blind & Dyslexic (RFB&D) and Harvard Medical School. He received his doctorate in learning disabilities from the University of Wisconsin-Madison. He is past-president of the Association of Higher Education and Disability (AHEAD) and former secretary of the National Joint Committee on Learning Disabilities. He can be reached at LBrincker@aol.com.

For Bill and Alissa

ACKNOWLEDGMENTS

I am very grateful for the help of the many people who supported me as I wrote this book. Special thanks to Kristin Stanberry, Marcelle White, Dr. Marshall Raskind, and all the other folks at Schwab Learning for their continual encouragement and content consultation as I conceptualized and wrote and rewrote. There were a number of people who lovingly "watched my back" on this project, reading and critiquing chapters where I wanted to be sure I had my facts right. Thanks to Jim Sarno of the Massachusetts Department of Vocational Rehabilitation; old friend Francine Kollias from Social Security; Dr. Robert Mulligan, Director of Special Education, Point Pleasant Beach, New Jersey School District; Dr. Mark Griffin, Headmaster of the Eagle Hill School; and Dr. Paul Gerber, who has always encouraged my work on adults and teens with LD. Candace Cortiella of The Advocacy Institute was incredibly generous with her time and expertise as I refined the text. Thanks, too, to my colleagues at the Threshold program at Lesley University (with an extra nod to Fran Yuan and Carole Noveck for their critiques), who have worked so hard over the years to identify transition needs and to provide exceptional service to young adults with LD.

Deepest thanks to Dr. Loring Brinckerhoff for writing the fine chapter on postsecondary options that appears in this book and to Princeton Review editor Suzanne Podhurst for her ongoing support and advice.

I'm extremely fortunate to have an extended family that has been tremendously encouraging throughout the writing of this book, particularly my daughter, Alissa, and husband, Bill, who is ever-patient and always so loving.

The Charles and Helen Schwab Foundation wishes to thank Arlyn Roffman for giving us the opportunity to contribute to this life-changing book. We appreciate and admire her sincere dedication to helping teens with LD make a successful transition to adulthood—both through this book and through her daily work. We also acknowledge our staff members, Dr. Marshall Raskind, Marcelle White, and Kristin Stanberry for their expertise and guidance in preparing this book.

CONTENTS

FOREWORD

The fact that you are holding this book in your hands suggests that you're one of several million parents raising a teenager with a learning disability (LD). It's a safe bet too that you've been especially worried about this time in your child's life—the transition to adulthood and the "real world"—since that first moment you noticed your child struggling to learn.

As a parent of a child with dyslexia, I understand the issues that may be keeping you awake at night. And, as a person with dyslexia, I fully appreciate the challenges that LD presents in moving beyond high school to college, vocational training, the workplace, and ultimately day-to-day living. Over the past decade, parents who visit our Foundation's website, SchwabLearning.org, have passionately voiced concerns, to my wife Helen and me, related to these transitional life events.

Our Foundation was pleased when The Princeton Review invited us to partner with them in the development of this book because we know how much it means for parents to have trustworthy guidance and support. The book, *Guiding Teens with Learning Disabilities: Navigating the Transition from High School to Adulthood*, is filled with just the right combination of expert advice, practical recommendations, and research-based information, along with personal anecdotes from parents and teens. I'm optimistic that the book will become a go-to guide as you and your teen look forward to this exciting stage in his or her life.

Over the next few years, I expect that you'll turn to this guide time and again. With each new challenge, I encourage you to remember that as your child prepares to meet his or her future, it will be in the company of millions of other people with LD who are contributing to the world in all sorts of extraordinary ways.

Charles R. Schwab

Founder, Chairman and Chief Executive Officer

The Charles Schwab Corporation

INTRODUCTION

From the time a child takes his first steps, he is working his way toward a life independent of his parents. By adolescence, psychologists refer to this quest for autonomy as *individuation* and note that it is the job of a teen to distance himself emotionally from those who raise him. This often involves establishing physical and psychological boundaries with parents (hence the closed bedroom doors and refusal to share any but the most superficial information) and at least temporary rejection of their ideas and values. None of this feels very good to parents, though many find it helpful to know that this behavior is normal—even healthy!—and that beyond this adolescent schism generally lies the eventual emergence of an adult-adult relationship.

Nonetheless, parenting through the adolescent years is a challenge. Behind the hormones and social angst, there are wonderful things happening for your child—including a leap forward in the ability to understand abstract concepts, development of identity and a personal moral compass, and an increase in physical strength and skills. But for most parents, the positive changes are offset by many worries, particularly about life beyond the school years. Will my son be able to make it in college? Will he find a job in which he can flourish? When will he have the skills he needs to take care of his own apartment? Will he be able to learn how to drive a car? Will he ever be able to manage a budget?

As the parent of a teen with learning disabilities (LD), you may find these questions keeping you awake at night. Unfortunately, there is reason for concern. Delinquency rates are too high among teens with LD, and both adolescents and adults with LD seem to be at greater risk of developing problems with substance abuse. Nearly 40 percent of adolescents with LD drop out of high school (U.S. Dept. of Ed.). Of those who graduate, parents expect only 59 percent to do so with a standard high school diploma (Cortellia). As they move into adulthood, individuals with LD face significant employment-related challenges—far too many are unemployed or under-employed—and many remain dependent upon their parents much longer than their non-disabled peers.

Despite these unsettling truths, there is reason to have hope for your child with LD. Much has been learned over the last few years about the factors associated with successful adjustment to adult life. The first, and perhaps most important factor, is having a supportive family—which your teen clearly does, since you have taken time to seek resources to guide you on your journey.

The Emotions Associated with Parenting a Child with LD

As the parent of a teen with LD, you have probably experienced a broad array of emotions over the years. For instance, you may have felt:

- *Grief* that your child is not who you expected him to be and that he has to suffer because of his disability.

- *Anger* that he has to work so hard at what seems to come relatively easily to others, and that he faces derision from people who don't understand the scope of his problems or appreciate the effort it takes for him to cope.

- *Resentment* at the amount of your time he consumes and at the fact that his school isn't doing more to help him succeed.

- *Jealousy* during conversations with other parents whose children seem to be so much easier to raise.
- *Relief* that there is a diagnosable disorder behind his various difficulties and that approaches and strategies are available to help him.

Such emotions are both normal and common among parents of children with LD. They only become unhealthy when parents allow them to damage their relationship with each other or when they are expressed as anger toward their child because of his disability.

Now that your teen is beginning his transition to adulthood, it is normal to experience concern about his future as well as sadness that his childhood is coming to an end. Keep in mind that although it is time to step back in some respects, you still have an active role to play. You will help him successfully navigate the transition to independence in the months and years to come and in will surely provide continual parental love and guidance as he settles into adult life.

What is *transition*, and why a book about this topic?

Adolescence is a time of many transitions for every teen, not just for those with LD. Some transitions involve a change in role, such as moving from passenger to driver, or from student to employee; others are physical, such as the onset of puberty or initiation of sexual activity. Still others are social, as teens decrease time spent with parents and center their social lives on peers. All of these changes are normal, yet each is stressful.

For teens with LD who reach age sixteen, the term *transition* has added meaning; it is a legally mandated process (see

Chapter 3 on transition planning) wherein the school and family work together during the development of a student's Individual Education Program (IEP) to prepare for life beyond high school. This formal process focuses on improving the student's academic and functional achievement to facilitate movement from school to post-school activities, including postsecondary education, vocational education, employment, adult services, independent living, and community participation.

The transition planning process is meant to address many of the concerns you and your teen have about his future beyond the K–12 years. Transition planning is a responsibility *shared* among you, your child, and your child's school; however, many secondary schools fall short in managing this responsibility well, and far too few families understand what they can expect in planning their child's future. This book will help you negotiate the often thorny formal transition process. It provides:

- Basic background information about learning disabilities in adolescents and how LD may affect their ability to master the skills needed to succeed in adulthood.

- Specifics about *transition*, both as a developmental period and as a process embarked upon within IEP development.

- Details about the collaboration among school, family, and outside agencies that is meant to help your child prepare for adult life.

- Tips that you as a parent can follow to supplement the school's offerings and to make sure your teen is ready for life beyond his high school experience.

Chapter 1 provides a basic introduction to learning disabilities and details five steps adolescents need to take to cultivate the self-determination that is fundamental to successful adjustment to adulthood. The steps include developing an understanding of LD, self-awareness, self-acceptance, choice-making skills, and self-advocacy skills.

Chapter 2 addresses mental health issues, which are too prevalent among our youth with LD, who often experience low self-esteem, loneliness, depression, anxiety, and behavioral issues. It provides tips for parents on how to foster a psychologically healthy home environment for the whole family and describes mental health treatment options available to your child and to the whole family, if necessary.

Chapter 3 presents a detailed overview of disability law and the transition planning process mandated under the Individuals with Disability Education Act (IDEA). It provides tools to help you and your teen prepare for active engagement in the transition planning portion of the IEP meeting.

Chapter 4 describes the challenges encountered by teens and adults with LD as they transition into community life. It offers many suggestions for how you can help your teen learn to take care of himself, perform housekeeping tasks, prepare meals, become a responsible consumer and money manager, and travel from one place to another independently.

Chapter 5 describes the path to employment for teens with LD. It outlines legal protections as well as the pros and cons of self-disclosure on the job. It also lists steps your teen will need to take in order to gain employment, including: further developing self-awareness and self-acceptance; understanding why people work; becoming aware of the full range of career options; exploring careers; developing prevocational skills; and assimilating into the work world.

Chapter 6 presents the various postsecondary options available to young adults with LD. You will read about the process of searching for, applying to, and selecting the appropriate college to attend based on your child's needs and the type and level of services offered. For teens for whom college is not the appropriate path, alternatives are discussed.

Finally, in Chapter 7 you will read about attributes common to successful adults with LD and about how you can foster development of the skills and attributes that will help your teen achieve a satisfying quality of life.

To easily access all of the SchwabLearning.org articles mentioned in this book, visit: SchwabLearning.org/teens.

Editorial notes from the author

Needless to say, both males, and females experience the full range of needs described in this book, but I have randomly assigned one gender to each chapter to avoid the awkwardness of the mixed-pronoun (he/she, him/her) problem.

Although I use the term *parents* throughout the book, I recognize that many teens are being raised by other adults, such as grandparents or guardians. Please read the word *parent* as inclusive of all caregivers in a parental role. In a parallel vein, I use the term *teens* throughout the book, knowing that some students with LD in transition are actually 20 or 21 years old; please read the word *teen* inclusively as well.

I have tried to make my explanations straightforward and thorough so that they might be helpful for parents across a range of experience; I regret if some content is too basic or too complex for your own level of knowledge and experience, but hope that it will be of assistance.

Finally, I hope you come away from reading this book with optimism about your child's future. There is a great deal that you can do—and that you're already doing—to facilitate his successful transition. Your task now is to help him build on his strengths and move one step at a time toward independent adulthood.

CHAPTER 1

UNDERSTANDING YOUR CHILD'S DISABILITY

WHAT IS A LEARNING DISABILITY?

There is no universal definition of a learning disability (LD). Even now, there is much debate about what LD is, how to identify it, and how best to treat it. We do know that LD is not a single disorder, but rather a diverse group of disorders that affects reasoning, processing, memory, communication, and basic academic skills—and is often manifested differently by different people.

While no single definition has succeeded in capturing the numerous and varied dimensions of LD, two stand out because of their comprehensiveness and relative levels of general acceptance. The National Joint Committee on Learning Disabilities, which meets twice yearly to discuss and issue reports on LD-related topics, settled on their most recent definition for LD in 1994.

The National Joint Committee on Learning Disabilities' definition is...

...a general term that refers to a heterogeneous group of disorders manifested by significant difficulties in the acquisition and use of listening, speaking, reading, writing, reasoning, or mathematical abilities.

These disorders are intrinsic to the individual, presumed to be due to central nervous system dysfunction, and may occur across the life span. Problems in self-regulatory behaviors, social perception, and social interaction may exist with learning disabilities but do not, by themselves, constitute a learning disability.

> Although learning disabilities may occur concomitantly with other disabilities (e.g., sensory impairment, mental retardation, serious emotional disturbance), or with extrinsic influences (such as cultural differences, insufficient or inappropriate instruction), they are not the result of those conditions or influences.

Having a clear definition of LD is crucial not just for practical purposes, but also for legal reasons. In order for the rights of students with LD to be *legally* safeguarded, a comprehensive definition—one that specifies *whom* the law protects—had to be created. Accordingly, the Individuals with Disabilities in Education Act (IDEA 2004) established the legal parameters of LD.

The Individuals with Disabilities Education Act (IDEA 2004) defines LD as ...

... a disorder in one or more of the basic psychological processes involved in understanding or in using language, spoken or written, which may manifest itself in an imperfect ability to listen, think, speak, read, write, spell, or do mathematical calculations.

Still other definitions suited to their own particular purposes are used by adult agencies, such as state departments of vocational rehabilitation. Although the many definitions vary in emphasis and wording, all agree that

- LD is a neurological disorder.
- It is a dysfunction of the central nervous system that affects an individual's ability to receive, effectively

process, store, recall, and/or transmit information to others.

- It causes seemingly unexplained difficulty in acquiring basic academic skills essential for success at school and work, and for coping with life in general.

Various committees and government agencies are in agreement that the learning problems associated with LD are *not* primarily the result of:

- Visual impairments.
- Hearing impairments.
- Motor impairments.
- Mental retardation.
- Emotional disturbance.
- Cultural factors, environmental or economic disadvantage, or limited English proficiency.

Most importantly, LD is *not* a disease. As such, there is no known "cure." There are, however, strategies and accommodations that make it possible to compensate for and cope with the associated challenges. This book will show you many tactics you can use to help your adolescent with LD successfully navigate the transition to adulthood. To begin, this chapter will provide an overview of the causes and characteristics of LD and outline strategies you can use to foster the development of self-determination and self-advocacy in your child.

CAUSES OF LD

LD is the result of a neurobiological dysfunction that affects the brain's ability to receive, process, store, and express information. Genetics can play a strong role: In many families, multiple members struggle with similar patterns of strengths and challenges. It is not uncommon for parents to discover their own LD upon learning the results of their children's evaluations. Many report experiencing an "a-ha!" moment and describe thinking, "Well, I had that same problem in school. You mean I could have had learning disabilities all these years?"

Charles Schwab, one of the first top executives to go public with his learning disability, has said that he only discovered that his condition—difficulty with reading—had a name when his son's dyslexia was diagnosed. The Charles and Helen Schwab Foundation has since launched SparkTop.org, an interactive website geared toward helping children with learning difficulties recognize their strengths and showcase their creativity.

Charles Schwab. "Kids Quiz Charles Schwab about the Personal Side of Learning Disabilities."
SchwabLearning.org/teens

Pre- and postnatal factors also seem to have an influence on development of LD. Poor prenatal care, substance abuse by the mother during pregnancy, problems associated with premature delivery, low birth weight, oxygen deprivation during or after delivery, and environmental toxins have all been cited in studies as causal factors.

CHARACTERISTICS OF LD

LD is a mix-and-match phenomenon; no two people with learning disabilities have the exact same set of characteristics. Each case is like a fingerprint, highly individual, with its own particular combination of areas of impairment and strength. Often, these characteristics—as manifested in weakness in basic academic skills, oral communication problems, or perceptual deficits—indicate the presence of LD, and ultimately bring a student to the referral process for testing and possible services. So, what are those symptoms?

1. Academic skills deficits

It is often a student's academic skill deficits that lead to referral for psychoeducational testing and possible services. Students with LD typically have problems reading and writing. In fact, it is estimated that 80 percent of children with LD have reading difficulties (Lyon, Shaywitz, and Shaywitz). These reading difficulties are often referred to as *dyslexia*.

- Reading: Many have difficulty decoding words, reading with fluency, and comprehending text.

- Writing: Many have difficulty translating their ideas from abstract thought to written form; organizing their thoughts; sequencing their ideas; using grammar, punctuation, and spelling; editing and proofreading to catch mechanical difficulties.

Difficulty with math, also known as *dyscalculia*, is also common among individuals with LD.

- Math: Many find math unusually challenging and regularly transpose digits (e.g., write *21* instead of *12*); fail to line up numbers properly while calculating;

omit steps when completing math problems; make careless calculation errors; have difficulty with mental math; and become confused by math-related vocabulary and concepts.

II. Oral communication problems

Individuals with LD often struggle with problems related to oral communication, receptive language, expressive language, or both.

Receptive language involves understanding what others say and finding meaning in speech and words. Those who have difficulty in this area are slow to process what they hear, become confused by figurative language, and are often left behind in a conversation that involves fast banter.

Expressive language problems make it difficult for individuals to convey their thoughts through the spoken word. They may speak in a non-fluent manner and struggle to find the proper words to convey their thinking.

III. Perceptual impairments

Perceptual terms are commonly used by educators and clinicians to describe some of the difficulties experienced by persons with LD. It is important for parents to be aware of and understand these terms. However, despite commonly held beliefs, research has not found many of the discrete perceptual deficits discussed here to be the primary cause of specific LDs. Perceptual deficits fall into four main categories: auditory, visual, spatial, and temporal. They are not related to acuity— people with visual perception problems, for example, may have 20/20 vision and still have difficulty discriminating between similar-looking shapes or objects; likewise, they may have perfect hearing yet struggle with processing what they are told.

Auditory

- *Auditory discrimination* involves differentiating between similar sounds. Individuals described as having problems in this area find it hard to hear the separate sounds within spoken words and have difficulties pronouncing polysyllabic words or learning foreign languages.

- *Auditory figure-ground* involves picking out necessary and relevant sounds from incidental background noises. People described as having a deficit in this area may have trouble listening to a conversation when there is interference from other sounds, such as pencils being sharpened within a classroom or dishes clanking and loud music playing within a restaurant.

- *Auditory memory* entails storing and retrieving upon demand what a person has heard, including phone numbers and homework assigned orally. People with an auditory memory deficit are likely to have difficulty remembering all of the steps in complex directions.

Visual

- *Visual discrimination* is the ability to distinguish between objects, sizes, and shapes, including letters and numbers. Problems in this area include *reversals (b-d, p-q), inversions (6-9), and transpositions (31-13)*. It is important to note that many people continue to believe that reading disabilities are the result of visual perceptual difficulties, such as the in ability to adequately discriminate between letters and letter sequences. However, the latest scientific evidence indicates that the real problem is a phonological deficit—difficulty in the ability to effectively process the specific sounds of language (Lyon, Shaywitz, and Shaywitz).

- *Visual figure-ground* involves focusing on a particular figure within a busy visual background, such as one word in a dictionary, one phone number on a page in a phone book, one country on a map of Europe, or one item on a blackboard covered with text or math problems.

- *Visual memory* involves storing and retrieving on demand what a person sees, including sight words (words that are recognized as whole words rather than being sounded out). Individuals with visual memory problems often spell sight words with the correct letters in the wrong order (such as *siad* for *said*) and struggle to remember the faces of new people they meet.

- *Visual-motor skills* involve coordinating vision with the movements of the body or parts of the body. They are often the major factor behind poor handwriting, messy cutting, and clumsiness on the dance floor.

Time and space

- *Temporal perception* involves understanding time. People with a deficit in this area often plan poorly and miss deadlines because they lack a sense of how much time it takes to complete a task. Similarly, because they underestimate how long it takes to travel to a destination, they often arrive late.

- *Spatial perception* entails relating sets of objects in space to each other or to oneself. Spatial problems often lead individuals to lose their belongings, confuse right and left, or get lost. A deficit in this area can also account for the poor handwriting of *dysgraphia*, a difficulty that results in letters and words being too tightly grouped or poorly organized on the page.

IV. Related issues
Other deficits

- *Executive functioning* is the cognitive process involved in planning, organizing, sequencing, and prioritizing. People with LD who have a deficit in this area have a tendency to be disorganized and routinely lose their belongings and manage their time poorly. They may have trouble knowing where to start a project, frequently fail to complete tasks in a timely manner, and often report feeling overwhelmed.

- *Social skills deficits* have a significant impact on the lives of many individuals with LD, both in and out of school. Individuals with LD often have difficulty making and maintaining friendships and are socially rejected by others. Although social imperception is not considered a primary characteristic of LD, it is listed here because of the high incidence of social issues among children, teens, and adults with LD. Specific social difficulties may include lack of appropriate eye contact; insensitivity to others' thoughts, feelings, and personal boundaries; weak conversational skills; frequent interruptions of others; and/or speaking too loudly.

Attention Deficit Hyperactivity Disorder

Many individuals with LD also have attention deficit hyperactivity disorder (ADHD). Although the focus of this book is on teens with LD, the main characteristics of ADHD should be mentioned, since between 25 and 50 percent of individuals with ADHD also struggle with symptoms of a coexisting LD (Silver 2006). The symptoms of ADHD may also hinder a student's success.

- *Distractibility* is a limited ability to tune out such internal stimuli as thoughts, hunger, pain, and sex drive, and such external stimuli as noise and movement. Those who struggle with distractibility often complain of feeling extremely vulnerable to unwanted thoughts that make it especially difficult to sustain attention to a task or conversation.

- *Impulsivity* is a lack of restraint that produces immediate reactions without forethought. Impulsive individuals often interrupt others, blurt out comments in classes and meetings, and respond too quickly in anger.

- *Hyperactivity* is persistent, heightened, and sustained activity levels that are inappropriate to the particular situation. While young children may literally climb the walls as a result of their hyperactivity, adolescents are more likely to exhibit a general restlessness by clicking pens, drumming fingers, or even talking too much.

In my book, *Meeting the Challenge of Learning Disabilities in Adulthood*, Glenn Young, former Learning Disabilities and Adult Education Specialist at the U.S. Department of Education's Office of Vocational and Adult Education, describes the complex mix of characteristics that make up his LD and coexistent ADHD:

...I reverse words and letters when I see them...often say the opposite of what I'm meaning, [for example] *yes* for *no*...often cannot recall the label or word or title of an object or cannot recall the name of the person standing in front of me, even though they may be my next-door neighbor. There are moderate to severe recall issues. I...cannot transform thought into written form and have severe handwriting problems. I also have classical left-right hemispheric conflict, where I don't always know left from right. I get lost in space. I have poor depth perception.

In addition to that, I have attention deficit [hyperactivity] disorder. LD tends to be more defined and is a neurological issue, whereas ADHD is more described as a neurochemical issue. So you have different manifestations as a result of different issues. I've worked very hard to control the manifestations of AD[H]D. If you knew me ten years ago, the manifestations were much more out of control— *extreme* hyperactivity; flitting from thing to thing; constantly appearing to be in chaos; an inability to focus in for a long period of time or becoming absolutely hyperfocused on something and not being able to break from it; extreme levels of energy and then extreme collapses. I could be completely on for something for days and then have to go into hyper-space for days or hours on end, often (with) a very severe lack of perception of what is going on around me socially and mechanically, often missing a lot of cues of how people are responding to me and not understanding their response (Roffman 2000, 11–12).

Despite his significant problems, Glenn has led a rich and independent life. He has earned a master's degree and has held a variety of professional positions. Keeping Glenn's story in mind, it is important for you to note that there is much room for optimism—that despite the challenges of LD, with careful planning your teen has every reason to look ahead to a positive future.

THE YIN AND THE YANG OF LD

Fuel for that optimism comes with the recognition that a learning disability comes with both a *yin* and a *yang*. Along with its challenges, or the *yin*, come strengths and talents, a *yang* that too often goes unacknowledged. For example:

- As a direct result of their own longstanding struggles, many people with LD develop deep compassion and empathy for difficulties faced by others.

- Many exhibit extraordinary drive and a determination to do well despite the challenges faced along the path toward their goals. With this determination often comes tenacity that helps them stick to what needs to be done, even if doing so requires more time for them than for someone without LD.

- In their quest to find ways to work around their weaknesses, many people with LD devise unconventional strategies to master routine tasks, and in the process develop creative problem-solving skills as yet another strength. This *learned creativity* (Gerber et al. 1992, 483) allows them to generate new ideas and think "outside the box," a valuable gift for anyone.

Coping With the Challenges of Learning Disabilities

There is no medication that reduces the symptoms of LD itself. If your child has co-occurring ADHD, she may find her concentration improved by Ritalin, Adderall, or other such drugs designed to reduce distractibility and improve focus. If she has co-occurring depression, a well-selected pharmacological treatment will likely lift her mood. For individuals with a primary diagnosis of LD, however, the treatment of choice is *education*—about the disability; their own profile of interests, strengths, and challenges; their legal rights; the modifications and accommodations that will enable them to succeed; and how to go about asking for those modifications in school, work, home, and in the community.

Fostering Self-Determination in Five Steps

As adolescents grow older, they seek increasing control over their lives and expect to be able to determine such matters as what they wear, with whom they hang out, how they spend their time, when they do their homework, and how they spend their money. Although their decisions are sometimes controversial to their parents—many require a round of discussion and an ultimate compromise—the decision-making process itself is central to their development into adults capable of leading independent lives. Helping your child learn how to problem-solve and make choices is crucial to her growth. This capacity is called *self-determination*.

Development of self-determination is essential to successful life adjustment, and we should actively teach teens with LD how to be self-determined individuals so that they may thrive as adults. Developing self-determination in people with LD is a multistep process that involves developing a general understanding of learning disabilities and building self-awareness, self-efficacy, and self-acceptance based on that understanding. With this foundation, it is possible for self-determination to flourish so that the individual is ready to step forward and self-advocate as needed. Once your child knows what she wants and needs and can ask for it, she will be better prepared to cope with her LD in a variety of settings, with a variety of people, and will be able to do so with strength, power, and increased self-esteem.

Step one: Developing an understanding of LD

In order to fully comprehend the specific profile of her own LD, your child must first understand what the term *learning disabilities* means. In all likelihood, she has lived with the label for years without fully understanding the basics of LD.

It's time to demystify LD for your child. Above all, she must know that LD is *not* mental retardation and that, while it *is* a brain dysfunction, there are strategies and accommodations that will allow her to lead a full and productive life. Perhaps she's heard about some of the famous people who have thrived with a learning disability—including scientists (Thomas Edison), politicians (John D. Rockefeller), community activists (Erin Brockovich), financiers (Charles Schwab, Richard Branson), athletes (Bruce Jenner), musicians (Cher, Jewel), actors and entertainers (Orlando Bloom, Patrick Dempsey, Danny Glover, Whoopi Goldberg, Woody Harrelson, Salma Hayek, Keira Knightley, Jay Leno, Henry Winkler), and designers (Tommy Hilfiger).

She also needs to know that there are teachers, coaches, plumbers, and all sorts of less celebrated folks out there who have prospered despite their LD, and that with careful planning, she can thrive too.

Parent tips for fostering an understanding of LD

Talk with your child. Ask her to tell you everything she knows about LD. Listen quietly and without comment as she speaks. Tell her you would like to work with her to fill in the chart below (Figure 1). The first column to be filled in is "What I know about LD." Everything she says should be written down, even if it is incorrect information, such as "LD means a person is stupid." If she needs help, work with her to fill in the second list under the heading, "What I'd like to know about LD" with any questions she might have about what an LD is or about how it manifests itself. Direct her to Internet sites such as LD.org, where, by clicking on "Living with LD," she will find a wealth of information specifically targeted to adolescents. Have her write the answers to the questions she listed in the second column under the heading, "What I've learned from my research." Discuss how her answers confirm her prior knowledge or respond to her questions about LD.

FIGURE 1: LEARNING MORE ABOUT LD

What I know about LD:

What I'd like to know about LD:

What I've learned from my research:

Make sure your teen has the chance to read and discuss the definitions of LD found earlier in this chapter or in the course of her Internet exploration. She should read through the basic characteristics of LD, and if she's willing, discuss them with you, focusing on how they have an impact on individuals both in and out of school.

A note about this exercise: Adolescence can be a trying time for any parent-child relationship, LD notwithstanding. If your teen is less than eager to sit with you and complete this activity, try talking through it when you have some quiet time together—perhaps in the car. Encourage her to tell you what she knows and would like to know about LD, and suggest how she might go about learning more. Later you can ask how her research went and perhaps share related tidbits from your own investigations of this topic. Avoid the temptation to conduct this research for her—it's important for her own growth and sense of self that she problem-solve to find the answers to her questions.

Step two: Developing self-awareness

Once your teen has a basic understanding of learning disabilities in general, she will be ready to start learning more about her own specific LD profile. Before embarking on that aspect of her journey to adulthood, though, she will need to learn more about herself by asking, "Who am I? Who am I within my family? Who am I among my peers? What do I enjoy doing? What am I good at in school, at home, in my community? What kinds of things am I less good at?" Once she has answered those questions, she is ready to add, "I know I've been diagnosed with a learning disability—what exactly does that mean in terms of my strengths and weaknesses in school, at work, and in the community?"

In the best of worlds, school personnel sit and talk at length with children who have LD and help them develop this level of self-awareness. They report their observations and the results of psychoeducational testing conducted as part of each child's special education assessments. The person who conducts the evaluation—generally a school psychologist or qualified counselor—discusses the assessment findings with those who have been tested and helps them develop an understanding of strengths and weaknesses unearthed during the course of the evaluation process. The person conducting the evaluation provides clear recommendations based upon the findings, including any special services, accommodations, or modifications needed, and why they are necessary.

Unfortunately, too few schools devote adequate time to this process of elucidation, and too few children with LD truly understand their disabilities. Even when the time for such meetings is set aside, however, it is often difficult for children with LD to grasp the information shared, in part because there are so many complex terms and concepts covered in this kind of discussion, in part because there is such emotional weight in messages about one's deficits, and in part because individuals with LD generally need important information repeated multiple times and in multiple ways to process, remember, and absorb it.

It's important, then, for parents like you to review and reinforce the information with your child. Make an appointment for you and your teen to sit down with her special ed teacher to review the profile of her strengths and weaknesses so that you'll feel confident that you understand the information and are prepared to discuss the results with her periodically at home. Also plan to review this information with your child before her annual Individualized Education Program (IEP) meetings (discussed at length in Chapter 4); doing so will help her understand and participate in the team's discussions.

Parent tips for raising self-awareness

Adolescents learn much about themselves through drawings, poems, timelines, photo montages, and targeted exercises, such as the one seen in Figure 2 below. Encourage your teen to fill in the chart to help her see that she has strengths as well as weaknesses and that she is already aware of some of the strategies that can help her succeed at tasks.

FIGURE 2: IDENTIFYING STRENGTHS, CHALLENGES, AND INTERESTS

What I'm good at:
What I'm not so good at:

What helps me do better:

_____

_____

What I like doing and would like to do
more often:

_____

_____

_____

Ask your child's teachers to direct her toward literature about individuals who have learning disabilities and Internet sites with information targeted to children, teens, and adults with LD. SchwabLearning.org/teens and LD.org are two sites that will help raise her self-awareness.

Learn enough about your teen's disability to be able to discuss it clearly with her. Give her opportunities to talk about its impact both in and out of the classroom setting. You and the school can collaborate to help her learn to work with her strengths and around her weaknesses whenever possible.

Many students with LD are unaware of the modifications made by teachers that enable them to succeed in class. By high school, it is important that your teen become well informed about all accommodations and modifications that have made a difference for her. Following high school graduation, she will need to self-advocate for such changes in work and postsecondary learning settings. Make sure your teen is fully informed about the modifications made on her behalf.

Step three: Developing self-efficacy and self-acceptance

Reassure your child that people with LD are not the only ones who experience failure—that, in fact, we all fall short and face disappointment at times. She needs to know that the key is to keep trying—that there is tremendous power in effort. Hard work does pay off, and through diligence and persistence, your child will be able to achieve many of her goals. Too many individuals with LD attribute their successes to luck—so it is up to parents and teachers to help them develop *self-efficacy*, the expectation that they will be able to achieve their goals and the understanding that their successes are, in fact, a direct result of their determined efforts.

It is normal for adolescents to be dissatisfied with themselves. One hates her nose; another is embarrassed by her acne; a third bemoans her shyness. In addition to these typical adolescent concerns, teens with LD often despair over their learning problems. Paul Gerber and his colleagues (1992, 481) report that it is very important for people with LD to *reframe* how they think about their disability, to think about it less negatively and even, if possible, to accept it as a positive element in their lives. Eighteen-year-old Jack is reframing when he declares, "I wouldn't give up my LD even if I had the power to get rid of it. It's part of who I am and makes me strong. Because of my LD, I understand people who struggle in all kinds of ways, and because of my LD, I have learned how to work around all sorts of problems. I consider those bonuses!"

Those who are able to perceive their LD as only a piece of who they are—who are able to *compartmentalize* their LD—will be more self-accepting and better situated to succeed in the adult world (Raskind et al. 2003, 226).

> *Every child has islands of competence, or areas of strength.... Resilient youngsters are able to articulate and use their strengths. Stated somewhat differently, they do not perceive their entire personality as associated with their learning problems.*
>
> Dr. Robert Brooks. "How Can Parents Nurture Resilience in Their Children?"
> SchwabLearning.org/teens

Parent tips for promoting self-efficacy and self-acceptance

Giving your child responsibility from an early age (e.g., having her put her games away after playing with them) fosters self-efficacy. As she grows older and increasingly capable, add to her chores and responsibilities.

Teach your teen to not be afraid of failure, either in or out of school. Help her see there is much to be learned from her mistakes.

☞ Model positive thinking about the mistakes you make by speaking your thoughts aloud in "think-alouds" (e.g., "Okay, so I burnt the cake. That happens sometimes. Next time, I'll be sure to set the timer, double-check the oven temperature, and keep a closer eye on what I'm baking.").

☞ Talk with your teen about trying to minimize academic competitiveness whenever possible. Encourage her to "run her own race," and help her understand the concept of going for her "personal best." Reinforce those values by refraining from comparing her to other kids and by reminding her of how far she's come.

☞ By late high school your teen should be self-aware enough to complete the chart in Figure 3. You and she should copy the chart, fill it in independently, then discuss what you've each written. Keep your charts for reference at discussions with her special education teacher or at her IEP meetings.

FIGURE 3: STRENGTHS, CHALLENGES, AND COPING IN VARIOUS SETTINGS

	School	Work	Community	Social Life
Strengths				
Challenges				
What helps				

Step four: Fostering choice-making skills

A major task of parents of adolescents—*any adolescent*—is to begin letting go. This is particularly difficult for parents of children with disabilities, who see their children struggling with an array of academic and social challenges and sometimes failing to develop skills needed for a successful launch into adult life.

Some parents underestimate the ability of their teenaged children with LD to make their own decisions. As a consequence, they continue to control their adolescents' lives, a practice that limits the development of self-determination, problem-solving, and self-confidence—all of which are so essential to successful adjustment to adulthood. Admittedly, it's not always easy to know where to draw the line on control when raising teens, but parents who do too much for their children and excessively restrict their opportunities to make decisions foster what is known as "learned helplessness" (Seligman 1972, 407), a passivity that significantly compromises the growth of skills essential for adult functioning. As a parent, you can help your child develop confidence and a sense of efficacy by starting to offer her opportunities from an early age to voice her opinions and participate in decision-making. This must not be an empty gesture, however—it is important that you be ready to listen and convey that her input will be valued. Let her know that, although you will not always agree with her or decide as she suggests, you will compromise if she makes a sound suggestion and will support the goals she sets.

Self-determination entails planning for one's own future by making choices, setting personal goals and striving to meet them, evaluating outcomes, and adjusting knowledge, goals, or plans accordingly. Your teen should be encouraged to voice her preferences about many aspects of her daily life, with the proviso that her safety and personal well-being cannot be compromised, and with the promise that her opinions will be discussed and respected while final decisions are made. When she enters into the transition planning phase of her IEP meetings, it is particularly important that your teen be able to convey her own vision of how independently and with whom she would eventually like to live, the type of job she would like to seek, and the ways she would like to spend her leisure time.

Parent tips for fostering choice-making skills

Experiencing the freedom to face challenges and make decisions helps build self-efficacy and ultimately, self-determination. By the end of middle school, your child should have considerable experience with open-ended choice-making (e.g., deciding what to make herself for lunch). She should regularly participate in planning her days under your guidance: determining when she should get up, listing the activities in which she will participate, and planning for meals and breaks. By late middle school, she should be able to assume responsibility for practical decisions (e.g., thinking through which books she needs to carry around in her backpack before lunch, which she'll need after lunch, and which ones she'll need to take home to do her homework). By the end of high school, she should have developed confidence in her choice-making ability and feel capable of making a variety of independent decisions.

Discuss adult life with your child. Listen carefully as she expresses interests and dreams about her future. Assure her you'll support her interests and that you'll help her take the necessary steps to achieve her goals.

Work together with your teen to set specific rules and limits, and clearly establish the consequences of falling out of line. Write down the rules, and be consistent about the consequences you set (e.g., "If you forget your lunch, you will have to buy one or go hungry that day; I will not deliver it to school for you."). If your child will benefit from repetition in order to internalize the rules, review them regularly.

Help your teen establish and maintain her own study habits and schedule (even if her study style involves multitasking, which makes no sense to you!), with the proviso that she is expected to complete and turn in all work and earn acceptable grades.

Involve your teen in decision-making related to her disability, specifically regarding her IEP, therapy, and accommodations at home and school.

Step five: Developing self-advocacy skills

Once your teen has developed self-understanding and tuned in to her own strengths, weaknesses, and needs for accommodations or modifications, it is crucial that she develop the ability to convey this information to others. Accommodations and special services are an entitlement during the K–12 school years; however, after your child leaves secondary school, it is only through self-advocacy that she will be able to secure the accommodations she needs to function well on the job or in postsecondary learning.

Your teen's secondary transition services should include a curriculum that fosters self-understanding, self-determination, and self-advocacy. She should not leave high school without being able to describe her strengths and weaknesses and how she is able to work around the areas of challenge she describes. Seventeen-year-old Lauren, for example, has role-played job interviews for day care positions in her school's resource room. She has practiced to the point where she feels comfortable telling an employer, "I love kids. I'm patient and caring and especially enjoy doing art projects with them. I have a learning disability that affects my reading aloud, but I do fine if I have a chance to take the book home and practice reading it. I'm very dependable, and have great follow-through if I have a chance to write down directions that have lots of steps."

There are pros and cons to consider regarding whether and when to disclose a learning disability to an employer or to acquaintances. Many times individuals with LD choose not to disclose their learning disabilities until people have had a chance to get to know them first. (This topic will be presented in greater detail in Chapters 5, on postsecondary learning, and 6, on work.) If and when your child does opt to disclose her LD, she should be equipped to self-advocate for needed accommodations and modifications.

Parent tips for developing self-advocacy skills

Make sure your teen has developed a written profile of her learning style, strengths, and weaknesses, as well as the ways she can work around her areas of difficulty. If she has not created this kind of document at school, encourage her to ask her special education teacher for help in doing so. This is a document that will have long-term value after she exits secondary school and begins her adult life.

Discuss this learning profile with your child. If her transition program has not included practice in self-advocacy, urge her school to add this component to her curriculum. Encourage your teen to role-play with her teachers (and with you, if she's willing) explaining her strengths and challenges to others, including to employers, instructors, or even bank personnel. It is hard to anticipate in advance to whom she might need to speak about LD-related challenges, but it's to her benefit to be prepared to speak up as needed.

Help your teen learn how and when she can discuss the challenges she experiences with others. Discuss the issue of self-disclosure and how the decision to disclose or not to disclose will vary based upon circumstances.

SUMMARY

It's important that your child develop an understanding of LD and the specific profile of her own learning disability. As she grows older, it is essential that she have increasing opportunities to make choices about her life, and that she take more control over how she handles the symptoms that challenge her both in and out of the classroom. It's crucial that she have a voice in how she handles the day-to-day decisions that shape her life. All of this can only be accomplished within a culture of respect for her and for the self-determination she is working to develop.

Self-determination and self-advocacy skills are essential to adult life adjustment for individuals with disabilities. An important outcome of developing these skills is increased preparedness to take control over what affects their lives. There is a positive correlation between higher levels of self-determination and better quality of life in people with disabilities, so concentrate on this with your child—it is truly of utmost importance.

CHAPTER 2
MENTAL HEALTH
AND WELL-BEING

Adolescence is a trying time under the best of circumstances. For teens with learning disabilities, the daily and lifelong struggles of coping with their disability-related symptoms can be wearing and dispiriting. Repeated failure, taunts from peers, and negative feedback from teachers often come at a considerable psychological cost.

PSYCHOLOGICAL SYMPTOMS

Many youth and adults with LD develop what is known as *emotional overlay*, secondary psychological issues that must be addressed along with the primary characteristics of LD. Although emotional overlay does not always develop into a major mental health problem, the psychological symptoms are very real and can be extraordinarily draining. This chapter will help you identify the psychological symptoms of emotional overlay in your child and will suggest various treatments to address them.

Low self-esteem

Your teen with LD may be very bright, yet as a result of his LD-related struggles, believe himself to be far less capable than he actually is. Many individuals with LD attribute their failures to being "dumb" and their successes to being lucky (instead of attributing it to their having talent or working hard). Their feelings of inadequacy are the unfortunate byproducts of chronic failure, of frequently being misunderstood by others, and of lowered expectations by family members and teachers alike.

Small Triumphs

Sixteen-year-old Brian complained that he had been left out of the dinner clean-up rotation in which his other four siblings participated in his home. His parents had felt he would not be able to load the dishwasher or do a thorough job of scrubbing the pots due to his learning disability. Although they had thought they were doing him a favor by excusing him from this task, their lowered expectations served only to decrease his self-efficacy and make him feel less capable and marginalized within his family.

After consulting with me, his parents began teaching him the step-by-step process of scraping the dishes and then loading the dishwasher.... After he mastered rinsing and loading the dishwasher, they taught him how to scrub the pots and pans. Once they committed the time to training him properly for this important life skill, Brian felt like more of an equal within the family, and then joined the chorus of his siblings' complaints about having to do this chore!

Many individuals with LD find it hard to recognize that they have strengths that offset their areas of challenge. When I asked nineteen-year-old Ashley to make a list of what she was "good at" during a session early in her work with me, she was unable to identify even one area that was positive. Happily, that changed with therapy over time as she progressed and developed greater self-understanding, self-efficacy, and self-acceptance. Now in her early twenties, she counts among her strengths that she can act, knows how to cook a delicious stir-fry, is an academic "plugger," and can create a beautiful beaded necklace.

For some individuals with LD, feelings of inadequacy are so deeply ingrained that they simply expect to fail at all their endeavors. They devalue the opinions of those who believe in their potential, and find it difficult to accept encouragement and praise. Based upon their history of academic struggles, they believe they will be unable to succeed, no matter how intense their effort, and wonder why they should bother to try at all. Many slip into a pattern of procrastination and fall short of finishing tasks both in and out of school to avoid what seems like an inevitably disappointing performance. There are a variety of steps that you as a parent can take to foster development of self-esteem in your child.

Parent tips for fostering development of self-esteem

Try to understand the experiences of your teen's LD journey. Be sympathetic about setbacks, commend effort, and praise hard-earned accomplishments. Celebrate the process ("I see how hard you're working on this report!"), not just the outcome.

Honest parent-teen communication is a protective factor against many mental health-related problems. Capitalize on every opportunity you have to communicate openly with your adolescent. Be candid with him about feelings of rejection and frustration you experienced at his age, and let him know that all teenagers—not just those with LD—share the misery of moments of self-doubt. Talk about coping strategies that did and didn't work for you, and suggest any that you think he might find useful. If you have a learning disability, share your story; you are in a position to be a great role model, as you're living proof that a person can succeed despite having an LD.

You may be fortunate enough to have a teenager who will readily express his feelings to you, but many adolescents are reluctant to share their emotional lives with their parents. Don't let that stop you from being attentive to your teen's emotional well-being. Watch for hints in his body language, and show compassion by reaching out either directly ("You look a little down—want to talk?") or indirectly ("I've been thinking about renting a comedy tonight—want to watch with me?").

Make sure that you have appropriately high expectations of your teen. Although it is not always readily apparent how high to set the bar, be aware that low expectations are far more damaging to self-esteem than the frustration of rising to challenges.

Liberally offer honest, clear, positive feedback, but only when it's warranted; he will begin to disregard earned praise if compliments are vague, too freely forthcoming, or less than genuine.

Reinforce positive behaviors with rewards that matter to your teen. Teach him to reinforce himself with self-praise ("Yay, I did it!"), activities he enjoys ("I get to go to the movies now that I got that task out of the way."), or new purchases, such as a CD.

It is not unusual for teens to lash out against their moms and dads since the parent-child relationship is often the safest in their lives. Expect that your teen's frustration and anger over LD-related difficulties may at times surface as blow-ups directed at you. Try to anticipate this dynamic and plan for it. When you're unhappy with your teen's behavior, make an effort to respond with patience and clear limit-setting that focuses on the specific changes you're seeking (e.g., "I can see you're upset, but I don't think it's with me—please talk to me with respect. Is there anything I can help you with?"). Although it's tempting to set punishments that take away favorite activities, be careful (as Janie's parents demonstrate in the following scenario) not to sacrifice one of your child's relatively few chances to display talent and to experience social success.

Care in Punishment

When Janie came home after curfew one night, her parents were tempted to restrict practice time with her band. Thinking it through, they realized that doing so would remove the major source of pleasure in her week, her one true period of relaxation, one of her few social opportunities, and the only arena within which she felt competent. They decided to limit her telephone use for several days instead.

It's important that your teen feel appreciated and accepted within the culture of both home and school. Check in with his special ed teacher to make sure that he is receiving positive feedback in at least some of his classes and in extracurricular activities.

Help him find ways to make a contribution in school and in the community. Encourage him to join at least one club where he can be a participant and perhaps assume some responsibility. Finding opportunities to participate in community service activities will help him build self-efficacy and confidence. Discuss the range of community service options, and help him identify the one that most appeals to him.

> In my research, I asked adults to look back at their childhood in school and describe one of their most positive moments involving something a teacher said or did to boost their self-esteem. The most frequent response was they were asked to help out or contribute in some manner, such as ..."I tutored a younger child," "I helped take care of the plants in the lobby." To be asked to help others communicates the message, "We believe you have something to offer and are a valuable member of the community."
>
> Dr. Robert Brooks. "How Can Parents Nurture Resilience in Their Children?" SchwabLearning.org/teens

Help your teen identify strengths and arenas in which he feels capable and can excel. If he's good with animals, for example, give him responsibility for pet care at home; if he's at all adept at sports, make sure he has a chance to participate on a regular basis; if he's technically savvy, ask him for computer assistance.

Encourage your child to engage in "calculated risk-taking" that might lead to new experiences and new competencies. It may take some exploration of different activities to find the one or two that fit him, but the process is important and worthwhile *and* has the potential to yield lasting interests that can be enjoyed throughout his adolescence and into adulthood.

Loneliness

A significant subset of children and adolescents with learning disabilities struggle with loneliness (Margalit and Al-Yagon, 2002). Although there are a variety of possible factors that can contribute to this emotional state, weak social skills may well be a primary cause. Students with LD tend to misinterpret social cues, struggle with social problem-solving, and experience more rejection or neglect by classmates than their non-disabled peers. If left unaddressed, childhood social problems persist into adolescence and have the potential to interfere with adult adjustment.

Many individuals with LD lapse into a negative cycle. They feel ashamed of their learning problems and withdraw from social activities; this prevents them from meeting others, a problem that further erodes their self-concept and makes them even less inclined to emerge from their isolation. As a result, they suffer from torturous self-doubt, and their self-esteem plummets. All of this can be far more interpersonally disabling than the LD itself.

Characteristics of LD often have social as well as academic implications. If your teen has *auditory processing* problems, for example, it may be difficult for him to discriminate between sarcasm and humor based on a speaker's tone of voice; similarly, if he struggles with *visual processing*, he may have difficulty distinguishing sarcasm from humor based on the person's facial expression.

Your child may stand too close to others, have poor eye contact, or have trouble modulating his voice volume in conversation with others. He may have difficulty grasping the concept of social boundaries and may not understand the unwritten rules of social pursuit. As a result, he may be too demanding or inappropriately open with new people he meets. All of this contributes to feelings of social isolation.

Case Study: The Impact of Social Skills Deficits

The wide-ranging effects of LD characteristics on the development of relationships are evident in the history of eighteen-year-old Molly, who came to me for help in dealing with her loneliness. Molly was a high school senior who, despite having a casual friend or two, often felt lonely. As we worked together in therapy, she came to realize the extent to which aspects of her LD had a social impact. She discovered that

- Her visual processing problems made it difficult for her to pick up non-verbal cues about when a conversation was over or whether a person was angry with her.

- Her auditory processing problems were an obstacle when she needed to tune in to one conversation in the cafeteria at school or at a party, where the sounds of music and laughing would compete for her attention. Whenever the noise level prevented her from tuning in to a conversation, Molly would smile and nod and hope others wouldn't notice just how lost she was.

- Her language processing problems made it difficult for her to understand jokes and idiomatic expressions; she coped by laughing and "faking it" so that others wouldn't notice.

- Her impulsivity led her to frequently interrupt others in conversation. While she recognized that this was annoying, insulting behavior and tried hard to wait patiently for others to finish their points, she often found herself flooded with thoughts that she could not wait to express, fearing she would forget them if she waited for a break in the conversation.

- Her tendency toward perseveration often led her to run on too long about her favorite topic, a particular television show she loved to watch. Failing to perceive cues that it was time to move on, she had been known to have listeners wander off in the midst of her monologues.

Molly was determined to alleviate her loneliness. We talked at length about her joining extracurricular activities at school and participating in youth group activities at church, but she wisely decided to begin becoming more socially involved by addressing the underlying social skills deficits that had always kept her from making more friends. She learned a variety of new skills that would help her break into new activities with greater potential for establishing new relationships. Each dealt with an aspect of her LD:

Visual processing: In therapy Molly read about body language and practiced interpreting non-verbal cues conveyed on clips from popular television shows. For "homework" between sessions, she wrote down examples of body language she observed and her interpretation of what the person was expressing. As a result, she became far more attuned to what people were telling her through non-verbal communication and was able to respond more appropriately in social interactions.

Auditory processing: Although she could hear perfectly, Molly learned to read the lips of speakers in noisy environments as a visual back-up to help her tune in more effectively to what they were saying.

Language processing: Molly decided to be honest with others when the symptoms of her LD would start to interfere with her interpersonal dynamics. She developed the habit of asking, "Could you say that in another way?" when someone would use figurative language that she didn't understand.

Impulsivity: Molly realized that interrupting was rude, but still found it hard to control this behavior. She decided to let her family members know she was working on this and asked them to cue her by holding up a hand when she started to interrupt them during conversations.

Perseveration: Molly asked her family members for their support, in this case, to let her know when she was going on too long about any one topic. Their cueing raised her awareness and helped her reduce her perseveration with others as well.

An additional concern arose regarding when and how to disclose her learning disability to new social contacts in her life. Molly worried that people would judge her, or that they'd think she was making excuses, but she decided that it was worth the risk to enable others to better understand her and the challenges she faced on a day-to-day basis.

There is much that you as a parent can do to help your teen combat loneliness and develop social skills.

Parent tips for fostering the development of your teen's social skills

Social skills training can be built into a student's IEP. If your teen needs to further develop his skills in this area, request that social skills training be included as a transition activity when he begins the transition planning process. A good social skills training program should accomplish the following:

- Foster development of the ability to express feelings and wishes to others.

- Teach how assertiveness differs from aggressive and passive behaviors.

- Help participants understand how to interpret the body language of others and how their own body language impacts their interpersonal interactions.

- Provide tips and role play practice in such skill areas as starting and maintaining conversations, giving and receiving criticism, asking for assistance, and saying no.

- Assign homework that requires them to practice newly learned skills in real-world situations.

You can foster your teen's social skills development at home as well. Talk with him about the fact that everyone has social strengths and weaknesses, and try to help him assess his own skills in this area. What social situations are most comfortable for him? Which ones make him feel uncomfortable? Does he feel relatively at ease starting and maintaining conversations with friends? With adults? Does he understand the body language of others? Can he adapt his own body language to fit various social situations? A word of caution:

Your child's perception of his own social skills may very well not match your own. Reinforce his social strengths and go gently down the path of bringing up any areas that need further development. Set a plan together of how to work on the skills that need attention. If he simply refuses to discuss this topic with you, suggest that his special ed teacher or guidance counselor address it with him.

Talk informally about some socials skills basics. For example, explain the importance of maintaining an appropriate distance—generally one arm's length—when speaking to others. If he has difficulty recognizing and interpreting non-verbal cues, make a game of observing body language on television and in movies you watch together. Turn off the sound, and discuss what the characters' bodies are communicating and what they may be feeling. Discuss how social expectations vary in different venues (e.g., at a dance versus at a graduation ceremony). Be proactive by anticipating and planning for novel or stressful social situations and by discussing social expectations ahead of time (e.g., "At your cousin's wedding, an usher will greet you at the door, will ask you if you're on the bride's or groom's side, and will let you know where you should sit.").

Once you've established specific target behaviors for your teen to work on, establish visual cues to alert him when his social behavior is slipping. But do be liberal with praise for his efforts to work on this very important area!

Depression

Although depression can be biological (i.e., a matter of internal chemistry), it can also develop as a reaction to a major stressor, such as the chronic academic and social difficulties that accompany a learning disability. The sheer day-to-day effort of coping with LD can be emotionally exhausting and can contribute to the development of depression.

Symptoms of depression are both mental and physical. *Emotional* symptoms may include a dejected mood, negative attitude, decreased interest in previously enjoyed activities, reduced involvement with people, crying spells, a diminished sense of humor, and sometimes unsettled, agitated behavior with quick arousal to anger. *Cognitive* symptoms may include difficulty concentrating, low self-esteem, pessimism about the future, indecisiveness, and a distorted body image. *Motivational* symptoms may include a loss of drive, avoidance, withdrawal, escapism, and increased dependency on others. *Physical* symptoms may include a change in appetite, sleep disturbances, decreased sexual interest, lethargy and fatigue, and restlessness or agitation.

Parent tips for dealing with depression

Watch for the symptoms of depression listed above. In addition, be on the lookout for any evidence of self-injury (e.g., "cutting" on his arms or legs, which is one way some teens attempt to release emotional tension).

Talk with your teen about your concern for his well-being, and encourage him to express his feelings. Many adolescents are more comfortable writing in a journal or on a computer weblog (*blog*) than speaking face-to-face with others about their emotions—suggest this option if he is not eager to sit and talk with you or any other adults.

Discuss your observations and concerns with your teen's pediatrician or with a mental health professional who has expertise in diagnosing and treating depression in adolescents. There is no blood test for depression, and evaluation takes time. Recognition of the problem is the important first step in treatment.

Since some cases of depression develop into suicidal thinking, have your child evaluated at once by a trained professional if he expresses hopelessness, despair, acute sadness, or morbid thoughts.

Often your teen will prefer for you to listen rather than offer unsolicited advice, which, no matter how well-intended, can feel like criticism to an adolescent. Unless the stakes are too high for you to step back and let him go without it, *ask* if he'd like your support or advice. If he says "no," sit back and just listen.

Acknowledge your child's pain, and offer sympathy when his heart is aching after a breakup. Avoid responding with platitudes such as, "There are plenty of fish in the sea—you'll find someone else special soon." Let him know that you can see he's hurting, that you are trying to understand what he's feeling, and that you are there to listen if he wants to talk.

Be empathetic, but exercise caution to avoid internalizing your child's struggles and riding along on his emotional roller coaster. Your role is to be supportive as he develops the skills and confidence to address his problems with decreasing parental involvement.

Talk with your teen's guidance counselor about any continuing concerns you may have. The presence of a caring adult at school protects against depression, so make sure your child is on the radar of at least one teacher or other school professional who can connect with him on a regular basis.

Stress and anxiety

Teens with LD often feel weighted down by the pressure of constantly having to cope with their symptoms. Some feel so apprehensive in the face of academic tasks that their anxiety is as much a barrier to success as their LD-related weaknesses. Yet their worries are not always limited to school work; they may feel acute stress about social as well as academic demands, with apprehension surfacing in the form of stomachaches, headaches, or a racing heartbeat. Many struggle with sleep disturbances—having difficulty falling and staying asleep or having recurrent nightmares. Adult education specialist Glenn Young describes one of his own bad dreams; it captures well the anxiety of living with LD:

> I was in a hallway filled with lockers stacked on top of lockers, endless rows of them. One of those lockers was mine, and what I needed in order to be functional for the day was in that locker. I had no idea which number locker it was, because I couldn't keep the numbers straight. There was an underlying sense of relief, because even if I could figure out which one of the lockers was mine, I would never be able to figure out the combination. This is a classic imaging dream of having the information and knowledge that you need in your head and an inability to get it in and out, and that's exactly what LD is about (Roffman 2000, 50).

As your teen moves through his high school years, he will experience increased stress about his future. Should he go to college? If so, to which schools should he apply? How will he fare on his SAT's? Will he be able to pass the high-stakes tests required in most states as a requirement for a regular diploma? If he is thinking about going directly into the workforce, what kind of job is the right match? Will he be able to find and keep a position? How should he handle questions about why he's not going to college?

Would you say anxiety is a problem for your child with LD and/or ADHD?

66%   Very much so

22%   Somewhat

5%   Not very much

3%   Not at all

0%   I'm not sure

Results are based on an online weekly poll of **SchwabLearning.org** readers.

The stress of decision making rises as adolescents move toward graduation. Tips for helping your child cope with these issues can be found in Chapters 5 (about postsecondary education) and 6 (about work). Below are some tips for helping him cope with the accompanying stress and anxiety.

Parent tips for dealing with stress and anxiety

Talk with your teen about stress and relaxation. Encourage him to fill in the chart in Figure 1 to help him identify typical triggers in his daily life (e.g., losing things, fighting with a friend), how they surface for him (e.g., as a stomachache or agitation), and coping strategies he could use (e.g., listening to music, talking with a trusted friend or family member). Discuss his responses, and refer him back to this chart when his stress level starts to mount. Support a routine (e.g., regular exercise) that helps him take charge and prevent stress from building up.

FIGURE 1: RECOGNIZING AND COPING WITH STRESSORS

Triggers	How I feel stress when this happens	What I can do to de-stress
Example: Losing things	Example: Get a headache	Example: Take deep breaths and mentally trace steps backward to remember where I might have left what Ive lost.

☞ Help your child understand that people can handle stress in one of two ways: By avoiding it or by tackling it head-on. Many withdraw from a source of tension, doing their best to avoid thinking about it at all. They procrastinate about completing tasks that must get done and do all they can to avoid stressful people with whom they must interact. Discuss the drawbacks of this approach, which is essentially a non-response, and model how to approach stressful problems directly.

☞ Use think-alouds to help your teen hear how you are strategizing about your own problems (e.g., "Ugh, I have to write that report for work this weekend. If I get right to it early Saturday morning, I can enjoy the rest of the weekend after it's done."). Encourage him to seek assistance and support from peers or family members when he faces problematic situations, feels stressed, and needs some help.

☞ When your teen is overwhelmed by a complex task, whether it's cleaning his bedroom or completing a major report for history class, help him reduce his stress by breaking the task into achievable chunks. A bedroom need not be cleaned all at once; he can pick everything up off the floor and put it into a pile and then tackle one section of the room at a time. Similarly, he can break down the large history report into manageable sub-goals.

☞ Look into whether your child's school provides the type of support described in the point above, often referred to as organizational tutoring.

Help your teen create order in his world. Encourage him to develop a master calendar on which all of his activities and responsibilities can be written. Suggest that he get into the habit of creating and using lists, which can be very helpful when breaking tasks down. Marking off each step as it's completed can be very satisfying.

Behavioral problems

In youth with LD, psychological problems—such as low self-esteem, depression, and anxiety—are sometimes associated with behavioral problems, such as juvenile delinquency and substance abuse.

Juvenile delinquency

There is evidence of a link between juvenile delinquency and LD. In 2003 the National Council on Disabilities estimated that approximately one-third of children in the juvenile justice system have learning disabilities. Although the research on this topic has not always successfully factored out emotional disturbance and behavior disorders from LD, and the actual numbers are not exact, we do know that juvenile delinquency is correlated with the low self-esteem, school failure, weak social skills, and impulsivity so prevalent among youth with LD.

> [It's important to remember that] even if we knew for certain that 30 percent of juvenile delinquents have LD, this does not mean that 30 percent of all children with LD will end up as criminal offenders.
> Dr. Marshall Raskind. "Research Trends: Is There a Link Between LD and Juvenile Delinquency?"
> SchwabLearning.org/teens

Substance abuse

Although there is no direct evidence that LD *causes* substance abuse or vice versa, the same low self-esteem, depression, and stress that put youth with LD at risk for juvenile delinquency create a risk for substance abuse. Like their non-disabled peers, many teens with LD use drugs and alcohol in an attempt to fit in socially, as an escape from their problems, or for a wide variety of other reasons.

Parents concerned that their children might be abusing alcohol or drugs should watch for symptoms, which include: a change in friends, self-isolation, staying away from home for long unexplained periods, lying, stealing, distinct changes in behavior, decreased school performance, exhaustion, red eyes, and a persistent cough.

For more information about learning disabilities and behavioral problems, visit the National Library of Medicine online at NLM.nih.gov.

Parent tips about behavioral problems

The suggestions listed earlier related to self-esteem will also serve to help prevent behavioral problems, such as juvenile delinquency and substance abuse. Although a teen with high self-esteem may act out or experiment with drugs, he will be less likely to fall into pathological patterns if he feels good about himself. Work with your spouse or partner to make sure you've established consistent rules and consequences for breaking them.

☞ Keep the lines of communication open with your teen, even if he is struggling with issues surrounding behavior problems. Dealing with criminal behavior in adolescents is a frightening proposition, but it is critically important that you remain communicative throughout any crises. Assure your child that you love him, that you're there to listen to his problems if he's willing to talk about them, and that you'd like to help him plan constructive ways of addressing them.

☞ If he falls into an abusive pattern with drugs or alcohol, arrange for substance abuse counseling with a professional who understands learning disabilities (see below for more on treatment). There are also numerous support groups targeted specifically to teens.

☞ Anticipate that your child may ask you about your own experimentation with drugs or alcohol. Prepare an answer; if you did experiment, explain why and talk about other mechanisms you might have used to cope with your problems.

Finding Treatment For Your Teen With LD

If your child is exhibiting mental health issues, there are various routes to accessing the help he needs, all of which begin with evaluation and diagnosis. A therapist should conduct a broad assessment that evaluates your teen's self-esteem and self-image, looks for learned patterns of behavior (e.g., learned helplessness), and uncovers any dysfunctional thoughts and feelings he may have. Assessment should include examination of interpersonal relationships with you, his siblings, and his peers, and it should evaluate his social skills.

Information regarding your teen's functional level within school, work, and the community is crucial to the process. Your teen may be found to have *co-morbid* (co-occurring) conditions, such as LD and depression or LD and anxiety. LD and ADHD are a common combination; less commonly, obsessive-compulsive disorder, bipolar disorder, Tourette syndrome, and conduct disorder are present in children with LD. If your child is diagnosed with one of these co-morbidities, it may be that his symptoms will be alleviated by addressing his LD first. If not, further treatment, including medications in some cases, will need to be considered (Silver, 2006).

In pursuing a therapeutic route for your child with LD, you may wish to consider individual therapy, group therapy, alternative therapies, or some combination thereof. You and your partner should work together with your child to determine the best program for him, given his needs and temperament.

INDIVIDUAL THERAPY

Psychiatrists, psychologists, social workers, and expressive therapists all work with individuals who have learning disabilities. The field of your child's mental health provider is less important than his or her background and understanding of LD. The clinician working with your child should have knowledge about the characteristics of LD as well as an understanding of the underlying issues affecting those with LD, including how it manifests itself in perception and self-esteem. An uninformed therapist can be misguided by some of the specific symptoms of LD.

Tales of Two Uninformed Providers

Jill's psychologist perceived her as resistant when she was consistently late for appointments; in reality her tardiness resulted from her poor time management. Jack's social worker underestimated his client's intelligence when he became completely befuddled by her question about how he was managing to juggle several balls at once on his job as a camp counselor. His reply, "What do you mean? I'm not a juggler!" had nothing to do with his IQ—it instead reflected a receptive language problem that makes it very difficult for Jack to grasp the meaning of figurative language.

If you are in search of therapy for your teen with LD, check that the mental health providers you are considering have the necessary background to recognize issues related to LD in adolescents. In addition, look for warmth and acceptance; it's important that the clinician be able to respond with empathy to the sadness, defensiveness, embarrassment, and anger your teen might be feeling at any given moment and be able to help him conquer his self-doubts. An added bonus is a sense of humor that can relieve tension as your child and the therapist work together on tough issues.

Beyond the above attributes, your child's clinician should also be able to make accommodations for learning disabilities during therapy sessions.

- If your teen has expressive language problems, the therapist should be extremely patient and encouraging as he tries to convey his feelings. The clinician should frequently double-check that she understands what he is trying to communicate by asking such questions as, "Is this what you mean?"

- If your child has a weak memory and writing difficulties, his therapist should write down the goals they set for the week.

- If he is stronger in his visual than in his auditory processing, his clinician might make use of pictures and diagrams to help him conceptualize particular therapeutic points.

Therapy with teens with LD should be practical, directive, goal-oriented, and focused on day-to-day issues. Your child will benefit from receiving feedback about his thoughts and behaviors, suggestions of coping mechanisms, and support as he prioritizes the steps he needs to take toward goals he and his therapist establish together.

Therapy should also incorporate relaxation training, particularly for those who struggle with anxiety. Your child should learn how to tune in to his body to recognize signs of mounting stress and be aware of various ways he can control tension (including listening to music, exercising, deep breathing, or soaking in a hot bath). He may find it helpful to call upon relaxing imagery (such as mentally hanging his worries on a worry tree just before going to sleep) or positive self-talk (such as saying to himself, "It's true, I have an exam tomorrow, and I could flunk. But I've listened in class, and I've studied, and I'll probably do fine").

GROUP THERAPY

Much may be gained by participating in group therapy which provides an opportunity for individuals with LD to see that they are not alone in their struggles. Group members with LD often benefit from sharing strategies and techniques related to organization, time management, and stress reduction. Your teen will have a chance to benefit from vicarious learning as others work on issues related to their own challenges.

Group therapy can be a particularly helpful approach for depressed or anxious teens with LD, as it provides an opportunity to discuss their feelings and to learn coping strategies from others without fear of ridicule or rejection. In a group, your teen may finally experience a connection with peers who share similar experiences.

Family therapy

A learning disability in one family member affects the entire family dynamic.

> At times, the whole family may be caught up in the whirlwind of adjusting to life with LD.
> Kristin Stanberry. "Marriage under Pressure."
> SchwabLearning.org/teens

Parents and siblings each respond individually to the challenges faced by the child with LD. It is not unusual for there to be tension between the parents and disagreements about managing their child's problems. Many times grandparents and other extended family members add to the strain, either siding with one parent, or contributing their share of unsolicited advice to the mix.

If your teen with LD has siblings, it is very likely that they—like you—have responded to his disability with mixed emotions. Many siblings feel a deep attachment and become fiercely protective of their brother or sister with LD. (In fact, a significant number become professionally motivated by their exposure to a disability within their family and ultimately pursue career paths that work toward the betterment of life for individuals with physical or mental challenges.) On the other hand, a large portion experience a degree of anger and resentment that their parents pay disproportionate attention to the child in the family with LD; that they themselves have to spend extra time helping, tutoring, or generally taking care of him; that the sibling with LD "gets away with a lot" in terms of his behavior, school performance, or contributions to the family chores. Some feel embarrassed, particularly if their brother or sister has poor social skills and is referred to by other kids as "retard" or "SPED."

There is much you can do to promote a positive family environment as you all adjust to LD in a family member.

Parent tips for promoting a positive family environment

It's extremely important that you share information about your child's LD in clear and simple language with each member of the family. Be open about his disability and about your hopes for his future. Your thinking will shape the attitude of your teen with LD and of his siblings; if you perceive LD negatively or view him as a burden, other family members are likely to adopt those perspectives as well.

> *One thing that stands out for me from my childhood is that my parents spent a lot of time educating me about my brother's LD. They helped me understand that he was struggling in school, not because he was stupid, but because he learned differently than I did. This helped me stand up for him and deal with it in a more positive way.*
> Katie, older sibling of a brother with LD, from "Learning Disabilities and Sibling Issues."
> SchwabLearning.org/teens

☞ Reserve one-on-one time with all of your children. Spending time alone with each child will help minimize siblings' jealousy of the many hours you need to devote to meeting the needs of your teen with LD.

☞ Teach your children the axiom, "Fair is not equal; rather, fair is giving each what he needs" and live by it within your family.

Siblings of youth with LD often benefit from voicing their feelings, but since it is not always easy for parents to elicit open, honest communication among their children, some families go to therapy together to help them achieve the goal of candid sharing. Family therapy provides a safe forum for communication and a chance to develop an understanding of the family's patterns of interactions and dynamics. Within the context of family counseling, each participant has the opportunity to express concerns, frustrations, and resentment. A clinician with a strong background in LD should be able to help all family members identify and understand the issues of the member with LD and learn how to deal with those that have a negative impact on the family unit. The group can work as a team to develop systems that will help life go more smoothly and improve family dynamics and patterns.

Team Punctuality

Sixteen-year-old Ron is a great kid who gets along well with his family, but his problems with time and space perception often lead him to get lost and arrive late to family functions. Many family events have been ruined due to his tardiness. His whole family was late to a Red Sox game once because he had miscalculated how long it would take him to get home after school. On another occasion, he got off at the wrong bus stop and was late for a family birthday party.

In therapy, his brothers expressed their annoyance at this pattern of behavior. They softened somewhat when they learned more about how his perceptual difficulties contributed to this problem, but they still let him know that they wanted him to change. His family worked out an arrangement whereby on the days when important events were scheduled, his mom would help him develop a written plan, working backward from the hour he had to be home and allowing plenty of time for travel. The plan would specifically include key details, such as the correct bus stop. One brother offered to serve as Ron's coach via cell phone. This teamwork proved successful—the incidence of Ron's tardiness diminished, and tension within the family was reduced.

Alternative approaches to enhancing mental health

There are other avenues to good mental health that may benefit your teen with LD. Many individuals find inner peace and develop greater self-understanding through yoga, meditation, or communing with nature. In addition, endorphins released through rigorous exercise effectively lift a depressed mood, relieve anxiety, and provide a general sense of psychological well-being.

SUMMARY

Many youth and adults with LD have secondary mental health problems, sometimes as a direct by-product of the LD-related challenges they experience. Feelings of inadequacy and low self-esteem may be internalized and develop into depression or anxiety. Loneliness is not uncommon, particularly among those who have social skills deficits. With the help of a well-trained, empathetic mental health provider or through alternative approaches to enhancing mental health, teens with LD can receive treatment that will alleviate their psychological symptoms.

CHAPTER 3
TRANSITION PLANNING

Transition planning is a process that will allow you and your teen to identify her next steps in terms of her continued learning, employment, and integration into community life beyond high school. Sometimes referred to as "future planning," this highly individualized, student-focused process is tailored to her particular needs, which are identified through formal and informal assessment, observation, and her own expressed vision of her future.

This chapter will clarify the legal and educational contexts of transition planning, help you anticipate what you may expect in the process, and offer tips that will help both you and your teen prepare to participate fully. After reading it, you should be in a better position to help her take advantage of services and accommodations to which she may be legally entitled under the law.

THE LEGAL CONTEXT

There are two major laws under which the educational needs of students with LD are generally met: Section 504 of the Vocational Rehabilitation Act of 1973 and the Individuals with Disabilities Education Act (widely known as IDEA 2004).

The Vocational Rehabilitation Act of 1973

Modeled after the Civil Rights Act of 1964, The Vocational Rehabilitation Act of 1973 (which has amendments dating to 1998) is a civil rights provision that mandates equal opportunity and nondiscrimination in all workplaces and educational settings that receive federal funding. Although Section 504 does not fund special education services, it nonetheless has clout since programs that fail to comply with the law—including private schools that draw upon federal funds for any purposes—lose government financing.

A person qualifies as disabled if she has a "major physical or mental impairment, which substantially limits one or more major life activities." Since learning and work both are considered major life activities, individuals with LD may be protected under Section 504 both at work and in educational settings.

To determine whether a child falls under the protections of Section 504, a multidisciplinary team (typically composed of the student, her parents, teachers, and counselor, the school's 504 coordinator, and special educators, as appropriate) conducts an evaluation of her educational needs. The evaluation takes into account her physical condition, social and cultural background, behavior, evaluations, and teacher recommendations. The team considers the student's disability, how it affects her education, and the services that will be most helpful. Parents are asked for permission to evaluate the child and are invited to be present at the meeting where a "504 Plan" is developed. The 504 Plan documents the *reasonable accommodations* the student needs—such as preferential seating, oral testing, and extended time when taking tests—to level the educational playing field. 504 Plans are re-evaluated periodically, and parents have the right to go to mediation if they disagree with the team's assessments.

The needs of students on 504 Plans are generally met through accommodations and/or modifications in the classroom. Those who require individualized instruction (officially termed *special education and related services*), however, may be eligible to be served under IDEA; if eligible, their Individualized Education Program (IEP), a more comprehensive document, generally takes the place of a 504 Plan.

Since students covered by IDEA are always eligible for a 504 plan, their IEPs should provide all needed services and supports—including accommodations generally provided under a 504 Plan. A graphic that clarifies the relationship between an IEP and a 504 Plan is available at WrightsLaw.com/advoc/articles/504_IDEA_Rosenfeld.html.

If your child is being served under Section 504, there is no legal requirement for her high school to engage in a formal transition planning process. However, even without an official process, your family could and should undertake systematic planning for her future. The remainder of this chapter will focus on IDEA, which mandates a formal transition planning process; however, even if your child has a 504 Plan, you may still seek assistance using many of the strategies and tips outlined in this chapter.

The Individuals with Disabilities Education Act (IDEA 2004)

Almost seven million school-aged children with disabilities qualify for educational interventions under the auspices of IDEA, which stipulates that qualified students with disabilities in grades K–12 are entitled to *a free and appropriate public education (FAPE)*. This means that schools must meet the needs of students with disabilities as well as the needs of those who do not have disabilities, and that they must do so within the *least restrictive environment*.

IDEA Eligibility

There are thirteen IDEA disability categories under which students may be found eligible for special education and services; Specific Learning Disability (SLD) is one of those categories. To be eligible for special education services under this category, a student must have an SLD, defined by law as "a disorder in one or more of the basic psychological processes involved in understanding or in using language, spoken or written, which may manifest itself in the imperfect ability to listen, think, speak, read, write, spell, or do mathematical calculations. Such term includes such conditions as perceptual disabilities, brain injury, minimal brain dysfunction, dyslexia, and developmental aphasia. Such term does not include a learning problem that is primarily the result of visual, hearing, or motor disabilities, of mental retardation, of emotional disturbance, or of environmental, cultural, or economic disadvantage." For more information about SLD requirements, visit SchwabLearning.org/teens.

The Individualized Education Program (IEP)

Under IDEA, services are detailed in an IEP, an annually updated, custom-designed legal contract created by a team composed of professionals, the child's parents, and the child herself. The IEP outlines the specific responsibilities of the school and the district with regard to the student's education.

In creating the written IEP, the team discusses and documents the results of recent individual evaluations, the child's strengths and weaknesses, parents' concerns, and the results of any state and/or district-wide assessments. The team notes the child's needs across a range of categories as well as how her LD affects involvement and progress in the general education curriculum. The student's academic performance and learning characteristics, social development, physical development, and management needs are all documented. The team determines a series of appropriate, measurable goals as well as the least restrictive educational environment for the child. It identifies the various special education programs and services needed to meet those goals, and notes the student's needs in terms of participation in assessments and testing accommodations.

The Office of Special Education Programs (OSEP) at the U.S. Department of Education maintains a website devoted to information and resources for IDEA 2004. The site is located at http://IDEA.ed.gov.

Under IDEA, if a family moves and a child transfers to a new school, her IEP travels with her, and there should be no interruption of services, including those related to transition planning.

The Transition Planning Portion of the IEP

IDEA specifies that "beginning no later than the first IEP to be in effect when the child turns 16," her school must augment the IEP development process by adding "transition planning" to prepare her for further education (if appropriate), employment, and independent living. According to IDEA, transition services are "a coordinated set of activities...designed to be within a *results-oriented process*, that is focused on improving the academic and functional achievement of the child...*to facilitate the child's movement from school to post-school activities*, including postsecondary education, vocational education, integrated employment (including supported employment), continuing and adult education, adult services, independent living, or community participation."

When IDEA was last reauthorized in 2004, several elements were included that are relevant to the transition planning process for your teen.

- Transition planning must allow her to work toward appropriate and measurable postsecondary goals that are developed based on age-appropriate assessments.

- Her IEP must describe the transition services and courses of study that will allow her to achieve the listed goals.

- The focus of her goals and of her transition planning process should not be limited to academics. Both should also include opportunities to hone functional skills needed for work and life within the community.

- All of this must begin as part of the IEP transition planning process for the IEP in effect when she turns sixteen, although the IEP team can choose to begin the process earlier.

SO HOW DOES THE TRANSITION PLANNING PROCESS WORK?

Although the transition planning process is tailored to each student's specific needs, the attendance list and agenda are usually consistent from one child's case to another's. The descriptions below should give you a sense of what you can expect as you begin the process with your own teen.

Who is on the IEP transition planning team?

- **Your child (the student)**

  Students are expected to attend as full participating members of the transition planning team or to document that their interests and preferences have been considered. Ideally, they should be ready to assume a leadership role at the meeting and be actively involved in decision-making regarding what goals are set and how and when those goals will be met. Unfortunately, far too few students both attend the meetings and take on a leadership role at them. Students tend to speak very little at their IEP meetings.

Has your teen led or participated in her or her own IEP meeting?

Yes   53%

No   47%

Results are based on an informal poll of SchwabLearning.org readers.

Even if your child is not ready to lead the discussion, she should be prepared to discuss her dreams and vision both for employment and for independent living. A plan for how to prepare her to participate in the meeting is included later in this chapter.

> *Participating in IEP meetings and following up with teachers and administrators to ensure [my daughter's] needs are met, taught her that many people have passed great laws to protect her, but that...[it] takes a great deal of skill and advocacy to bring [them] to fruition...[She] knows she must have the desire to learn and succeed in order to be successful, and that she will have to continue to work hard and recognize strengths and weaknesses in herself and others in order to network successfully and continue to advocate for herself throughout life, in her quest to be an educated successful adult and ultimately a happy adult. The IEP process has given her skill and ability in negotiating well beyond her sixteen years of age.*
> "Most Valuable Parent Club Survey."
> SchwabLearning.org

- **You (parent/guardian)**

  As her parent, you are the key expert on your child and are in a prime position to provide information about her strengths, interests, areas of challenge, independent living skills, and the kinds of supports she needs. Too few parents are actively involved in the IEP meeting; as a result, most IEP goals are ultimately determined by the school. It's important that you feel empowered to be actively involved, as you are a full member of the team and have much to add that will positively influence the IEP and transition planning process.

- **Special education teacher**

  The special education teacher is able to provide information from his or her vantage point about your child's strengths, weaknesses, achievements, progress made toward IEP goals, and teaching strategies that have worked well with her. The special educator will be able to help the team identify any needed related services (e.g., vocational school programs), suggest links to appropriate agencies (e.g., the Department of Vocational Rehabilitation), and begin the process of coordinating services and programs.

- **Local Educational Agency (LEA) representative (your school district)**

  A representative of your school district/LEA must attend the meeting. This representative must be qualified to provide or supervise the provision of specially designed instruction and must be knowledgeable about the general education curriculum and the availability of the school district's resources. Your LEA representative supports your child's special educators and classroom teachers, provides information about programs in her school and within your community, and allocates necessary resources, such as technology, and other accommodations and supports.

- **General education teacher**

  At least one of your child's general education teachers attends the meeting as well. This instructor helps identify appropriate postsecondary goals for your child and plan a general education course of study that will help her achieve those goals. The classroom teacher will be working along with the special education teacher to monitor your child's progress toward the goals included in her IEP.

- **Psychologist/professional who can interpret assessment information**

  The meeting may be attended by a mental health professional who is able to report and interpret the results of any new assessments that have been completed to identify your child's strengths, aptitudes, and needs. Often the person attending is the one who conducted the evaluation, but the results may be reported by one of the team members listed above. Whoever presents the results should also discuss recommendations based on the findings. Together the team should set goals that take the reported results into consideration. School guidance counselors are routinely part of the IEP team once transition planning begins, but only if invited. Check the list of those who have been invited on the meeting invitation letter that you receive from your child's school; if someone you feel is important to the proceedings is not on the list, you may request that he or she be included.

- **Other agency representatives (as appropriate)**

  Depending on the student's needs, representatives of community agencies, such as the Department of Vocational Rehabilitation or Social Security, may be invited to the transition planning meeting to help identify community and adult services that may support the transition process. Recent research indicates that too few schools bring agencies into this process; the Department of Vocational Rehabilitation and other agencies participate in only a fraction of IEP transition planning meetings.

  For students considering postsecondary learning, the Disability Support Services representative of the community college, college, or university she is interested in attending should also participate. IDEA permits participation by phone or video conferencing if the representative is unable to attend in person.

- **Advocate (as designated by you and your child)** You and your teen may elect to invite a trusted advocate to the meeting. This person may be a family friend, another relative, a former teacher, an employer, a professional advocate, or anyone else who cares about and is knowledgeable about your child.

IEP and Transition Planning Meetings are critical times in the lives of students with disabilities. The school districts and their special education personnel realize this. They also understand that your interest, investment, and concern regarding the future of your transitioning student is a priority. Sometimes emotions run high at these meetings and discussions become deadlocked because the participants fail to agree—often over minor points of difference. Recognize that these situations call for objectivity and an approach that is mutually accommodating. No single idea should be accompanied by the slogan: "My way or the highway!" There's always more than one way to do things effectively and efficiently. My advice is, don't walk out—work it out.

Dr. Robert K. Mulligan, Director, Special Education, Point Pleasant Beach School District, New Jersey

What is the agenda of the transition-specific portion of the IEP meeting?

At the transition-specific portion of the IEP meeting, the team will devise a coordinated set of transition activities to develop appropriate measurable postsecondary goals and determine the transition services needed to reach those goals. As you embark upon the planning process with the rest of the team, it will be helpful for you to have a clear sense of what to expect. What follows is a synopsis of each of the key areas of focus.

- **Identifying the student's future goals.** The whole transition planning process should focus on your teen's vision of her future. Prior to the meeting, she should be guided by you and her teachers through a series of conversations about *post-school outcomes*, the official term for what she would like her life to look like once she leaves high school. These discussions are designed to help her identify the path she would like to take and focus on answering questions you and she might have about her future day-to-day life. They will help clarify for her and for you such matters as in what setting and with whom she would like to live, what she would like to do with her free time, how she envisions herself participating in community life, what kind of job she would like to have, whether she would like to continue her studies, and other similar long-term aspirations. Decisions will depend on her personal desires, cultural background, the nature and severity of her disability, the extent to which she needs daily or weekly support and supervision, and available finances. Some of the key questions to consider are

○ **Where will she live?** There are a variety of living options to consider. Does she want to continue living with you? Would she prefer to live outside the family home? If so, would she like to room with others or live alone? If she is headed off to college, would she prefer to live in a dorm room or in an off-campus apartment—once again, alone or with others?

○ **What will she do in her free time?** Teens with LD often have difficulty planning their free time. Many choose leisure activities that are solitary, such as surfing the Internet or playing video games, and need to be guided and supported to look for group involvement. Lots of group extracurricular activities offer opportunities to become a team player, make friends, cultivate a talent, and have fun. Would she enjoy joining a community softball or Ultimate Frisbee team? Working out at a local gym? Singing in a community chorus? Taking an art class or participating in community theater? Discussing the many options will help her identify some that have personal appeal.

○ **What transportation will she use to access the resources of her community?** Is she interested in getting a driver's license? In many geographic areas, driving is the principal (if not the only) means of getting around. If having a driver's license will foster the necessary level of independence in your teen, then work together to develop a plan for her to get one. With planning, a license can be successfully obtained. If public transportation is the only viable travel option, will she need to learn to use it? As a person with a disability, she may be eligible to use special transit service by accommodated vehicles in your area.

○ **How well-developed are her daily living skills?** Does she need help learning to be more independent when she shops, goes to the movies, or eats out on her own? Is she able to do her own laundry? Can she manage her own medications and other health needs?

○ **What are her employment goals?** Most adolescents aren't ready to answer the frequent query, "What do you want to be when you grow up?" Nonetheless, many have identified interests that will help them begin to explore certain career paths. For example, your teen may know that she likes children but not know yet whether she'd like to be a teacher, a children's librarian assistant, or a day care worker. Or she may know that she likes working outside, but may not be sure what kinds of jobs would allow her to do so. The military is an additional vocational option for her to consider. Based upon her interests and abilities, she may benefit from supported employment, volunteer work in a field of interest to her, vocational training, or continuing her education.

○ **How will she continue to learn?** Is your child interested in attending college? If so, she may have specific plans, such as getting an associate's or bachelor's degree in a particular subject—or, she may have more general plans simply to get a degree and, ultimately, a job. Many students take a year after high school to work or travel; many don't attend college at all. Perhaps your teen is not interested in a degree but would like to become certified for specific work, such as plumbing. In many communities, there are post-secondary vocational school programs that may be accessed. Or she may want to take individual classes to develop such skills as car repair or desktop publishing.

To help your teen discuss her vision of her future at the meeting, it will be helpful for her to have filled out the questionnaire in Figure 1 before her IEP team meets. Bring the completed form to the meeting and have her refer to it with the rest of the IEP team. As she reports the answers to these questions, your fellow IEP team members will take note and work with you and her to create goals that will enable her to realize her dreams for the future. She may not need to work on aspects of every single domain; this process should help identify which need attention.

FIGURE 1

Student Transition Planning

Answer these questions before your meeting to help you participate in planning your transition goals.

Living

Where do you think you might like to live after you finish high school?

__At home

__Away from home (check all that apply)

    __Alone

    __With others

    __In an apartment

    __In a dorm on a college campus

Learning

Are you interested in continuing your education after high school?

__ Prefer to work/volunteer or pursue other goals

__ Yes

    What would you like to learn about?

    _____

Do you know where you'd like to study? (check all that apply)

__Near home

__Far from home

__At a community college

__At a large university

__At a small college

__In the city

__In a suburban area

__In a rural area

__Other preferences: _____

Working

Are you interested in going to work right after high school?

__ Prefer to pursue postsecondary learning or other goals

__ Yes

What kind of job would you be interested in?

_____

Do you want to work full-time or part-time?

__Full-time

__Part-time

Daily living

Which skills do you think you still need to work on in order to be able to manage on your own after high school? (check all that apply)

__ Cooking

__ Shopping

__ Cleaning

__ Managing money and paying bills

__ Doing laundry

__ Taking care of my medical needs

__ Taking care of my personal hygiene

__ Driving

Recreation/leisure

What do you like to do for fun?

_____

How would you like to spend your free time after you finish high school?

_____

Choices

What kind of choices do you make for yourself now?
(e.g., about clothes, free time, etc.)

_____

What other choices would you like to make for yourself
in the future?

_____

What do you need to learn to be able to make those
choices for yourself in the future?

_____

- **Discussing the student's Present Level of Academic Achievement and Functional Performance (PLOP).** Before appropriate transition goals can be set, the team needs to know your child's current level of performance—not only in academics, but also in functional areas, such as vocational, community, recreation and leisure, and daily living skills. The team should discuss strengths and weaknesses in each area, based upon ongoing assessment from special education teachers, general education teachers, vocational supervisors, and others involved in your child's education as well as from you and your child.

- **Establishing a "coordinated set of activities."** It is up to your child's IEP team to determine the transition services—the _coordinated set of activities_—that are needed to assist her in reaching her goals. These activities should be designed to build upon her strengths and work around her weaknesses, and they should be based on what she _can_ do rather than on what she _cannot_ do.

Goals and Supports

In the process of IEP development, the necessary supports can only be identified after your child's goals are determined. The team cannot limit itself to planning around preexisting programs for other students with disabilities within your school system. If a new service will be required to meet your child's needs (e.g., work-study programs or job shadowing), it is up to the district to provide it.

Once your child's transition goals are set, she should be assisted in choosing the courses of study that will help her work toward them. It is critical that she see the relevance of each course to her vision of her future; students who fail to perceive the point of their schoolwork are at higher risk of dropping out of high school. If she is planning to continue her education after high school, her curriculum should consist largely of precollege academics, and her goals should help her through the postsecondary selection and application processes. If she is interested in entering the work force and moving into an apartment with a friend right after high school, her transition activities should include life skills classes and vocational training.

Your child's plan should define each of the transition activities listed on her IEP, identify who within the school and/or in outside agencies has primary responsibility for each activity, and specify the dates when each activity will begin and end.

Given the areas in which your teen appears to need assistance, the team will establish her goals accordingly, in some cases providing transportation for IEP-approved programming. The following examples demonstrate how goals can be set for students based on their personal vision and PLOP:

Work: Julia told her team she would like to work with children who have learning problems.

 One of her IEP transition goals states that she will work as an unpaid intern for six hours per week at a day care center for children with special needs.

Community life: Nathan let his team know that he wants to help people in his community.

 One of his IEP transition goals is to volunteer at the local food pantry on Thursday afternoons.

Recreation/leisure: Manuela loves dance and other forms of exercise. She told her team she would like to fit physical movement into her free time.

 One of her transition goals is to look into available dance classes within the community and participate in at least one per week.

Postsecondary learning: At his IEP transition planning meeting, Mark expressed his desire to go to college and earn at least an associate's degree.

One of his transition goals is to investigate the disability support services and admissions requirements of a local community college and two universities.

Daily living: Bella has thought a great deal about her future. She announced to her team, "I'll live with my parents while I'm at community college. In a couple of years I'd like to move out and live in an apartment with a roommate. Later I'd like to get married and have kids and a dog."

One of her transition goals is to open and maintain a personal checking account and to set up a savings account dedicated to her future apartment needs.

Determining transition activities: *Transition activities* span (but are not limited to) the categories listed below. Note that your local district may offer alternatives to these specific activities. For example, although you may request cooking lessons at the local culinary institute, your child's district may offer available accommodations through the school system and propose to provide this training at the local vocational training program. If your child expresses interest or needs support in a particular area, make sure that it is present in some form on her transition activities list. Key areas include the following:

Instruction: Although instruction is typically school-based and traditionally takes the form of academic classes, tutoring, general education classes, and vocational/career classes, it may also be offered beyond the school campus by other agencies, such as a local community college. Transition activities listed under Instruction might include:

✔ Registering for an SAT preparation class in Grade 10.

✔ Applying for needed accommodations on SAT/ACT tests.

✔ Visiting colleges and meeting with their Disabled Student Services staff to investigate supports offered.

✔ Participating in a transitional program on a college campus.

✔ Taking a CPR or first-aid course.

Related Services: Your child's IEP team will determine if there are any supportive or therapeutic services and activities needed during or after school to help her achieve her goals. Related Services include transportation, physical therapy, occupational therapy, vocational rehabilitation counseling, mobility/travel training, and speech therapy. Transition activities listed under Related Services might include:

✔ Receiving assistance in applying for services from the Department of Vocational Rehabilitation.

✔ Receiving assistance in submitting paperwork to the Social Security Administration for transportation funding to and from work.

✔ Securing counseling to develop social skills needed on the job.

Community Experiences: Based upon your child's vision of where and with whom she would like to live after high school, the IEP team will consider her options regarding where she will reside and how she will become involved in community life. Preparation for participation in the community best occurs outside of the school in actual community settings, such as a bank, where the targeted skills can be put to real use. Transition activities centered on Community Experiences might include:

✔ Researching locally available apartments.

✔ Eating at local restaurants.

✔ Finding options of nearby gyms for working out.

The Importance of Authentic Assessments

Make sure your teen's school provides an ecological or authentic assessment that allows her to demonstrate her level of vocational and functional skills in a real-life context, not just in school. For example, rather than relying on a classroom-based test on money management, it is preferable that your teen be assessed as she handles money in a store or in a bank and, similarly, that her vocational skills be evaluated in a work environment.

Employment: According to preliminary findings of the National Longitudinal Transition Study-2 (Wagner, Newman, Cameto, Levine, and Garza, 2006), a highly respected research project following thousands of special ed students from as early as grade seven into adulthood, the primary transition goal of more than half of all students with disabilities is to gain competitive employment. Preparation for employment is a step-by-step process that includes career awareness, career exploration, career preparation, and career assimilation (each of these topics is covered more fully in Chapter 6). Your teen will work with her school or other agencies, such as the Department of Vocational Rehabilitation, as she advances toward employment goals.

A critical prerequisite to planning employment activities is a functional vocational evaluation, which provides information about a student's career interests, aptitudes and skills, and level of performance in actual work settings. This evaluation may be completed by school personnel or by outside agencies, such as the Department of Vocational Rehabilitation or the local vocational school program affiliated with your teen's public school. Transition activities in the area of Employment might include:

✔ Attending a career fair in Grade 11.

✔ Visiting the local office of the Department of Vocational Rehabilitation to check eligibility requirements.

✔ Completing the online application for vocational rehabilitation.

✔ Finding a paid job in a specific area of interest.

✔ Participating in job shadowing of two jobs in an area of vocational interest.

✔ Meeting with military recruiters to investigate vocational training within the various armed services.

Post-school Adult Living Activities: A good transition planning session should include a discussion about such matters as whether your teen plans to get a driver's license and eventually own a car. If so, a series of goals can be set that will help her work her way toward this goal.

Establishing a clear sequence for accomplishing long-term goals often proves very helpful. Consider the following example:

Joy will take her driver's permit test in Grade 9;

Joy will get her license in Grade 10;

Joy will investigate the cost of used cars and explore options for insuring a car in Grade 11;

Joy will purchase a used car within her budget in Grade 12.

Transition activities in the area of Post-school Adult Living might include:

✔ Registering to vote.

✔ Arranging for health care coverage.

✔ Learning to file insurance claims.

✔ Buying furniture.

✔ Renting an apartment.

✔ Investigating local medical care.

✔ Planning a vacation.

Daily Living Skills: Daily living skills are often taught in life skills classes. If a school is not prepared to teach a particular skill, such as cooking, the IEP team may suggest that this training be provided with available accommodations by the head of the district's cafeteria service, at a local vocational school program, in another public school that offers such a program, or even at a local agency.

> Juan wants to live in an apartment when he graduates, but his school doesn't offer any home economics classes. The IEP goal states, *"Juan will take a cooking class at the local community college, where he will learn to plan and prepare at least three breakfasts, three lunches, and three dinners."*

Transition activities focusing on Daily Living Skills include:

✔ Cooking.

✔ Shopping.

✔ Money management/consumer skills.

✔ Self-care.

- **Establishing how progress toward achieving transition goals will be monitored and reported.** At the IEP meeting, be sure to ask how your child's progress will be monitored, evaluated, assessed, and reported to you, and at what intervals all this will happen. IDEA 2004 does not require monitoring and reporting progress on transition goals, so your school is more likely to provide this information if you specifically request it.

PREPARING FOR THE PROCESS

You and your child should prepare for the IEP meeting in advance to help you make the most of the transition planning process.

Preparing your child for the IEP meeting

IDEA requires that students attend their IEP meeting once transition planning begins. If they do not attend, the school must ensure that their preferences and interests are considered throughout the process. To give your child the best possible preparation for her IEP meeting, you'll need to make sure that she has learned and is prepared to take an active role by self-advocating. Active engagement by students leads to more positive feelings about the entire process; everything will proceed more smoothly if your child is involved.

While the ideal scenario is for students to lead their own IEP meetings, it is the rare teenager with LD who is equipped to do so. However, it is very important that she participate to the maximum extent possible. Most teenagers with LD will be able to participate at least minimally if they have received explicit instruction in how to be engaged in the process. Providing a student with the self-advocacy skills needed to participate in and even lead an IEP meeting can be built into her IEP as a goal in the years leading up to the start of the transition planning process.

> I found that having my son [at the IEP meeting] "opened his eyes" as to the "importance" of education, and it even helped my son get a better understanding of the countless hours I've spent trying to research and learn and advocate for his needs.
>
> "Healthy11," message board post on SchwabLearning.org/teens

Parent tips for preparing your child for the IEP/transition planning meeting

☞ Although most teachers agree that a student's involvement is important, too many lack the training and time to make this a focus of instruction. Urge your child's teachers to make training in IEP participation a teaching priority, and refer them to StudentLedIEPs.org and *Student-Led IEP's: A Guide for Student Involvement* (available through the Council for Exceptional Children at CEC.Sped.org). Both are good resources on the topic of student engagement in the IEP process.

☞ Work with your child's school to help her prepare for the transition planning IEP meetings. Empower her with knowledge about the process itself. She needs to understand that the point of the meeting is to make a record of her strengths, areas of challenge, and goals— and then to devise an individualized plan for *capitalizing* on her strengths, *improving* her areas of challenge, and *achieving* her goals. Further, she needs to know about:

- The procedures of the IEP meeting.
- The IEP document and its purpose.

- Who attends the meeting, and why.
- The agenda of the transition-specific meeting.

☞ Assure your teen that her participation is both welcome and necessary. Let her know that the team will be receptive to her questions and suggestions about her needs and what she knows works well for her. Remind her that she should not feel pressured into making decisions she is not capable of handling, and that she has the option to step out of the room to discuss a decision in private with you or with any other advocate she may have invited for additional support. Ask her teachers to offer her the opportunity to role-play an IEP meeting ahead of time. As she role-plays with a teacher or advocate, she should especially practice:

- Introducing herself and the other team members.
- Stating the purpose of the meeting ("We're here to discuss my IEP, to get updated on how I'm doing, and to set transition goals for me.").
- Opening the discussion about her past goals and how she has progressed toward meeting them.
- Describing her academic and non-academic strengths, areas of challenge, and interests (what she likes to do now and what she'd like to do more of in the future).
- Expressing her vision for her future and participating in setting goals to achieve her dreams.
- Describing the types of supports she believes she needs to achieve her goals.
- Thanking the team members for attending at the close of the meeting.

My daughter was taught self-knowledge and self-advocacy...at her high school. Learning to participate in her IEPs gave her the confidence to advocate for herself in college. It gave her both the necessary skills and the knowledge that accommodations are her legal right. "Most Valuable Parent Club Survey."

SchwabLearning.org

Preparing yourself for the IEP meeting

Your best preparation for the transition planning process is to become an informed consumer.

Parent tips for preparing yourself for the IEP/transition planning meeting

 Familiarize yourself with how your school district approaches transition planning by:

• Contacting the director of special education, your child's case manager, or her special education teacher, and asking about the format of transition planning that your system follows.

• Asking if there is one particular individual in charge of the transition process in your school district, and requesting any forms that will help you think about the meeting in advance.

• Asking if there are other families who have gone through the transition planning process who would be willing to serve as your mentors; learning about their experiences with the school and community agencies will help you as you progress through your own process.

- Checking your state education department's website for state-specific information about transition and contacting your state's Parent Training and Information Center for guidance and information about transition planning.

At the transition planning meeting itself, you and your teen should consider yourselves full and equal members of the team. Providing your input in writing conveys your interest in approaching this process as an active, involved partner. If you are concerned about having adequate time to address transition planning thoroughly, you may request a two-part IEP meeting, with the second part completely devoted to the transition process. Look for a clear explanation of the results of any transition assessments and/or reports, and ask questions if you need clarification of any terms, results, or recommendations. Speak up with any comments you wish to add or with information that conflicts with what is presented. Your fellow IEP team members should work collaboratively with you, supporting you and helping you understand not only your child's legal entitlements and how the mandated transition process works, but also how to begin letting go of your teenager. To help you prepare to participate in the meeting, complete the questionnaire in Figure 2.

Parent Preparation for Transition Planning

Reflect on the following in preparation for your child's meeting:

Strengths I perceive in my child:

_____

_____

_____

Areas of weakness I would like to see the school address:

_____

_____

_____

My dreams for my child:

_____

_____

_____

What I feel would keep her from achieving these dreams:

Other concerns I have about my child's future:

Post-school goals I would like to see included in her transition activities:

Living

Where and with whom I envision my child living after high school:

Learning

Where I envision my child continuing to learn:

What I envision her learning:

Steps that need to be taken now for her to continue learning after high school:

Working

Work I think my child would both enjoy and do well:

Independent life

Skills my child needs to work on to have independence after high school:

___ Cooking

___ Shopping

___ Cleaning

___ Managing money

___ Doing laundry

___ Taking care of her medical needs

___ Taking care of her hygiene

Recreation/leisure

Recreation/leisure activities I think my child would benefit from learning:

_____

_____

_____

Choices

Types of choices my child makes now (e.g., about clothes, free time, etc.):

_____

_____

_____

_____

Further choices I'd like to see my child make:

_____

_____

_____

What she needs to learn so she may make those choices:

_____

_____

_____

☞ Keep in mind that the IEP team's mandate is to conduct student-focused planning based upon your teen's goals and expressed needs. Accordingly, the process centers on *her* wishes rather than *yours.* Difficulty at the meeting arises when the parents and the student disagree about future plans. For that reason, it is extremely important to keep the lines of communication open and talk at length about your teen's needs and wishes *before* the meeting, when you can take the time to come to an agreement. Ideally, you and your partner, your child, and the team can work together to devise a plan that works for everyone.

The better prepared you are, the better prepared you will be to help your teen ready herself for the IEP meeting and, ultimately, for the transition process. If you approach the meeting and future plans with a positive, can-do attitude, she is all the more likely to do the same.

In some cases, what's best for your child may not be immediate independence at the age of majority—eighteen in most states—but rather gradual progress toward an independent life. IDEA requires that no later than a year before your teen reaches the age of majority, she must be alerted about any rights that will transfer to her on her next birthday, and her IEP must include a statement that she has been so informed.

At the age of majority, she assumes legal control over her educational placement, educational records, eligibility, evaluations and programming, and any mediation or due process needed to resolve disputes. When she reaches this milestone and assumes her rights, the school must provide notices of upcoming meetings to her as well as to you, but all other notices will go to her alone.

It is not the norm, but there have been cases of students who, upon reaching the age of majority, have asked that all their special education records be destroyed. Others have signed themselves out of special education altogether. Again, this is the exception rather than the rule, but it is nonetheless crucial that you discuss the transfer of rights with your child ahead of time, and in particular emphasize both the importance of the responsibility she will assume and the long-term repercussions of her decisions.

Exceptions can be made to the policy of transferring rights at the age of majority if a student is not capable of making informed decisions. If you feel your teen lacks adequate judgment and decision-making skills, is unable to consider options or recognize the consequences of her decisions on her own, you may wish to investigate additional supports available through the courts. Guardianship, conservatorship, or another form of representation by an advocate may be appropriate.

- Under *guardianship*, an individual is deemed legally incompetent and loses the authority to make all the decisions granted at the age of majority. Beyond IEP-related rights, this includes the right to vote, apply for credit, and sign contracts. A guardian is assigned by the court to make critical decisions. Generally the parents act as the guardians, but when they are either not appropriate or unavailable for this role, another adult may be appointed.

- In some states it is possible to arrange a more limited guardianship, called a *conservatorship*, under which the individual is not considered legally incompetent and retains as many rights as the court determines appropriate. Again, the parents are the first in line to be named conservators. The conservator's decision-making responsibility is limited to areas carefully delineated by the court (e.g., solely in the area of money management).

A Case of Conservatorship

When she was just twelve, Maryann's parents died, leaving her a $200,000 trust fund. Her aunt and uncle raised this delightful young woman, who early on was identified with severe LD, and they always encouraged her development of independence. As she approached the age of majority, however, they were concerned that her math skills were very weak, that she had developed few money management skills, and that she didn't comprehend the buying power of her inheritance. They discussed their concerns with her, explaining that they felt it wise to become conservators because they wanted to

---

protect her from losing this nest egg. They assured her that the trust fund was still entirely hers but that becoming conservators would allow them to advise her about how to spend this money wisely. They would henceforth work as a team to make significant financial decisions, such as buying a car or a condo. In the meantime, she would receive a monthly allowance that would more than cover her expenses.

Petitioning for guardianship or conservatorship is a legal process. Keep in mind the significant limitations on your child's right to make independent decisions if you choose this route. Check your state law if you and your teen feel she is not ready to assume the level of responsibility required at the age of majority, yet is too capable to be declared incompetent. There may be procedures that will allow an advocate to represent her in a less restrictive arrangement.

Parent tips for when your child reaches the age of majority

Begin discussing the transfer of rights with your child as early as possible—even before the topic is addressed at her IEP meeting. Make sure she understands the rights that will transfer to her when she reaches the age of majority.

Help your child develop her own good working relationships with school personnel and other IEP team members so there is little disruption when she reaches the age of majority.

Stay involved even after you are no longer the primary participant in the development of your child's IEP. IDEA does not address parents' attendance at IEP meetings once a student has reached the age of majority. The school or student could, however, invite a parent to attend the meeting as an individual who is knowledgeable about the student's educational needs and abilities. Ideally, you'll continue to be actively involved in planning the services and programs for your teen's transition into adulthood.

GRADUATION FROM HIGH SCHOOL

Aside from reaching the age of majority, there are other circumstances that may have an impact on your child's educational path. Under IDEA, graduation from high school with a regular diploma is considered a change of placement. Schools are obligated to provide *prior written notice* that they are proposing to graduate a student who has disabilities with a regular high school diploma. You must be told reasonably in advance via a Procedural Safeguards Notice so you and your child have sufficient time to agree with or challenge the school's proposal and respond and prepare appropriately.

Some families struggle with this decision, since eligibility for FAPE ends when a student with LD graduates with a regular high school diploma. They very legitimately wonder: Should their child graduate with her class and end her entitlement to special services? Or should she take advantage of the fact that students with disabilities who continue to have transition needs may receive special services until they reach age twenty-two? Discuss the issue with your teen, preferably before you've received any notice. Some systems offer students the option of participating in the graduation ceremony and activities without receiving a diploma so they may take an extra year or more to focus more fully on transition goals; others will not allow the student to "walk" with their class unless they graduate.

For students who need to stay in high school beyond age eighteen to master academic and transition skills and meet the requirements for a diploma, some schools offer an "18-to-21-year-old program." Although designed, staffed, and overseen by high school personnel, programming is often located off the high school campus—at a local community college, for instance. As a result, the program isn't simply extending the high school experience, which would be unacceptable and embarrassing for most teens. The goal of "18-to-21-year-old" programs is to allow access to adult services and provide age-appropriate settings for needed transition services in the areas of employment, postsecondary learning, and community involvement. These programs also aim to promote the development of self-determination, social skills, and recreation skills.

Most states provide an alternative exit document, a certificate of completion or an alternative diploma, which verifies that a student has attended high school. You and your child should carefully consider the implications of earning an alternative diploma, as doing so places some restrictions on post-secondary learning or employment. As of this writing, some state colleges are accepting applicants with alternative diplomas, and some employers are hiring without distinguishing the type of diploma earned, but many graduates with disabilities find that their options are limited by not having a standard high school diploma. You should talk with your teen about her goals and abilities, and check whether she would be able to achieve what she's set out to do with an alternative diploma. If not, work with her and her IEP team to establish a track that will enable her to earn a standard diploma.

SUMMARY OF PERFORMANCE (SOP)

Before your teen's IDEA eligibility terminates, either upon graduation with a regular high school diploma or upon turning twenty-two, her school is required to create a *Summary of Performance* (SOP), that documents her accomplishments and transition needs. This document is required under IDEA 2004 but is not an official part of the IEP transition process—yet it is most useful when linked with the IEP and transition planning process. You may request that a review of the SOP and discussion about its contents be included in the IEP transition meeting.

States vary in terms of the depth of information required in the SOP. Although no new evaluation is required for the development of this document, the SOP must report the student's academic achievement and functional performance, and it must include recommendations of how to assist the student in meeting her postsecondary goals. This document must be specific, meaningful, and understandable to the student, the student's family, and to any agencies (including postsecondary institutions) that may provide transition services. (See Chapter 5 for more on the topic of postsecondary education.)

A helpful resource regarding the Summary of Performance is
http://vacollegequest.org/charting/performance_forms.html.

Summary

As the parent of a teen with LD, you have the right to expect that your child will leave high school prepared for her future with self-understanding, self-efficacy, self-determination, the ability to self-advocate, and the functional skills needed to manage adult life.

If your child is on an Individualized Education Program, the school has the legal responsibility to initiate transition planning in preparation for the IEP that will be in effect when she turns sixteen. Individualization is essential in this process. You should expect nothing less than a custom-designed plan based upon the goals developed to promote her vision of her future. Any course work planned for her should move her closer to the post-school outcomes listed on her IEP.

You can promote the growth of your teen's self-determination in the transition process by helping her prepare for IEP transition planning meetings; urging her to communicate her interests and preferences at the IEP meeting and letting her know that her voice is key to the process of creating an appropriate, individualized transition program; allowing her to participate in making key decisions about the IEP meeting, including who should be there and when the meeting should be held; and helping her learn about adult agencies so she can make an informed choice about which agencies to involve in her transition process.

CHAPTER 4
LIFE IN THE COMMUNITY

ANTICIPATING LIFE BEYOND THE FAMILY HOME

Most adolescents eagerly anticipate a more independent adult life. Like their non-disabled peers, many teens with LD feel ready to consider life beyond their parents' home and include "moving out" as part of their vision for the future during the transition planning process. Options for more independent living include remaining at home but with increasing independence, moving into a college dorm, renting an apartment or house alone or with roommates, buying a house or condo, or moving into supported living, where there are staff members who live in and provide some supervision.

To help your teen anticipate what his next steps will be, discuss his various options with him. If you can, sit down with him and work together to complete the questionnaires in Figures 1 and 2 of Chapter 3 on transition planning. If your adolescent is not inclined to join you in this formal exercise (as many would not be), then try to discuss these issues with him informally, perhaps during a quiet car ride together.

Regardless of when your child moves out on his own, he will benefit from developing the skills addressed in this chapter.

Background: The need for community life preparation

According to a variety of studies, young adults with LD participate less in community life and remain reliant upon their parents long after their peers have achieved independence. The National Transition Longitudinal Study-1 (Wagner et al., 1991), followed 8,000 special education students for several years into early adulthood. At the point when they were three to five years out of high school, only 27 percent of those with learning disabilities were found to be independently engaged in work or school, regularly involved in social activities, and residing outside their parents' homes. Only 50 percent were independent in even two of these arenas. Data from the second wave of the NTLS study suggest these trends are improving; nevertheless, there is clearly a need for our teens with LD to focus both in school and in the home on preparation for community life.

It should be noted that cultural norms, financial constraints, lack of confidence, and personal preferences keep many non-LD youth at home with their families for years beyond high school, in some cases until they are ready to marry. The trend toward extended dependence among youth with LD may be partially attributed to a lack of the necessary community living skills, as well as the tendency of some parents to assume too much responsibility well into adolescence (and beyond) for managing the lives of their children with LD. Although these overprotective parents mean well, their take-charge style contributes to "learned helplessness." When children have few chances for decision-making, they miss out on the opportunity to discover that they are even *capable* of making good choices or that much can be learned from failure. They are less able to develop the skills and self-determination needed to plan and fend for themselves, and this seriously limits their potential for growth.

Fostering independence

Teens need and benefit greatly from opportunities to make their own decisions and demonstrate independence. The following case histories describe two young women with LD—both nineteen years of age and high school graduates, both scoring similarly on measures of intelligence—and illustrate how different parenting styles can help or hinder a teen's development of independent living skills.

A Tale of Two Teens

One was energetic and outgoing and had led an exciting life during her teen years. She had a driver's license, had held several part-time jobs, and enjoyed spending her salary at the mall, which she frequented with her many male and female friends. She did her own laundry, made her own lunches, and occasionally cooked simple suppers for the evenings when she was on her own.

Her history stood in stark contrast to that of the second young woman, whose parents admitted to being "a little overprotective." This young woman had never been expected to assume any responsibility for chores at home; had never, in fact, even made herself a sandwich. She had never held a job, had neither a license nor friends. Even on her bicycle, she had always been restricted to the block on which the family lived.

Denied the opportunity to blossom, the second young woman was caught in the stranglehold of dependence. As soon as she had the opportunity to learn independent living skills, she grew enormously;

---

clearly, she had been ready to move forward toward an independent adult life. Her major constraint was not the learning disability itself, but the attitude of her parents who had cultivated a prolonged dependence. In contrast, the first young woman had been eased along with both high expectations and a great deal of support from her parents and had developed a number of skills that would serve her well as she left home and began life in her own apartment (Roffman 2000, 164).

Even with appropriate parental support of their need for increasing independence, teens with LD experience bumps in the road toward community living. These challenges often relate directly to the specific characteristics of their disability, and they may change over time, ebbing and flowing as the individual grows older and faces new demands in life. For example, difficulty writing a book report in high school may morph into difficulty filling out forms at the doctor's office in early adulthood.

During your child's school years, it is only natural that you have been focusing on the aspects of LD that have most affected his day-to-day life, in particular those that have shaped his learning experiences. But because LD is far more than simply an educational matter, and because its effects spill well beyond the classroom into day-to-day functioning at home, in the community, and on the job, your focus should now expand beyond the purely academic and into the functional realm.

Whether your teen's transition goals have him heading off to college or to employment, he, like all young people, must develop an array of community living skills to adjust successfully to adult life. The remainder of this chapter addresses a number of those skills, some of which are quite challenging for many teens and young adults with LD. With awareness of the potential for difficulties, careful transition planning, and explicit instruction in the areas of challenge both in life skills classes at school and under your tutelage at home, adolescents with LD *can* learn these skills and move successfully into community life. There's much you can do to help your child prepare.

KEY SKILL SETS

As your teen begins to plan an independent life, work with him to make sure he acquires the array of necessary daily living skills. Although some may seem mundane, they are nevertheless important to adult functioning.

Grooming and personal hygiene

Grooming and personal hygiene, which are so essential to social and employment success, may be compromised by a learning disability. For example, weak reading can be an obstacle to deciphering directions on products (e.g., hair gel) and equipment (e.g., electric razors). Fine-motor coordination problems can make it hard to use the hands and fingers effectively; this in turn may make shaving, tying a necktie, or applying makeup difficult—all of which may result in a rather disheveled appearance in some youth with LD.

Parent tips for teaching your teen about hygiene and grooming

By middle school, your child should know how to attend to his personal hygiene and be familiar with various types of personal products. By high school, he should be purchasing the products he prefers (e.g., razors, deodorant, shampoo) within an agreed-upon budget.

Buy an electric razor for your teen if he has fine-motor problems or spatial difficulties, and encourage him to double-check manually to make sure he has fully shaved the intended territory.

If your teen has visual discrimination problems, encourage him to enlist a friend or relative to act as a clothing advisor.

Encourage your child to keep his morning routine simple and to allow ample time for hygiene and grooming. Some find it alleviates morning stress to shower and lay out clothing the night before school or work.

If he is willing, urge him to establish a routine of following weather forecasts every night and setting out accessories (e.g., umbrella) appropriate for the next day's conditions.

LD and Housekeeping

Characteristics of LD often present obstacles to good housekeeping. For example, Sean, who has a visual-motor (eye-hand coordination) problem, tends to be clumsy when he washes dishes; and Ashley, who has spatial perception problems, has difficulty not only sweeping and vacuuming the floor thoroughly, but also setting the table with the utensils correctly placed.

Housekeeping

Adolescents aren't generally known for their housekeeping skills. It is quite normal for them to have a messy room with clothes and belongings strewn here and there. For teens with LD, life tends to be particularly disorganized and, without instruction in this area, their messiness can get out of control. Many adults with learning disabilities admit to ongoing struggles in their efforts to maintain a clean, organized, and functional living space. As a parent, you are a critically important resource for helping your teen develop the broad array of skills that will help him effectively manage a home.

Housekeeping entails a variety of skills that your child with LD can readily acquire if he is offered explicit instruction and supervised practice. Although he may not *ask* you to teach him to clean, rake, sew, or do the other chores mentioned in this chapter, he will be much better prepared for adult life when he has learned these practical skills. Furthermore, if you don't take the time to teach them to your child with LD as you might with your other children, he may feel all the more different and like a marginalized member of the family.

Parent tips for helping your teen learn to clean and maintain a household

☞ By adolescence your teen should have experience performing simple household tasks and be ready to take on additional chores. Creating step-by-step checklists for housekeeping duties will help him focus on one task at a time and avoid becoming distracted or feeling overwhelmed.

☞ During your child's middle and high school years, enlist his help in the kitchen. Explicitly teach him, step-by-step, how to clear dishes from the table and wash them by hand or load them in the dishwasher; how to fill the detergent dispenser and set the dial to the appropriate cycle; and how to wipe down the stovetop and counters. Later, teach him to return all washed items to the appropriate shelves and drawers.

☞ Introduce cleaning products and techniques for tackling the floors, toilet, sinks, and shower or bathtub. Make sure your child understands any key terms (e.g., "toxic").

☞ Demonstrate and talk your way through one cleaning task at a time, and then have him do as you've done. Verbally coach him through each task the next few times until he can complete it without your cues, and use think-alouds as you work (e.g., "I'm being especially careful to hold this vase as I dust it because it's so breakable" or "I'm using this kind of polish because the shelf is wood, but it would ruin the chrome table in the den.").

Model how to sweep or vacuum a small space methodically, thinking aloud as you go (e.g., "I'm starting at each corner and sweeping toward the middle so there'll be only one pile to pick up; then I'll know I've covered the whole floor."). Be patient as you observe your child practicing; while these tasks may seem simple to you, they present a very real challenge to those with spatial difficulties.

Recycling can be an art. Talk with your child about the rationale behind the recycling movement, and show him how to prepare recyclable items for collection or drop-off.

Tending to houseplants requires some understanding of how plants grow and thrive. Your adolescent should be able to care for a plant of his own. As he (and it) grows, show him how to remove dead leaves, fertilize, and re-pot his plant. If he demonstrates interest, give him responsibility for additional houseplants, and introduce outdoor gardening.

As an adolescent, your teen should be able to help with yard maintenance. Supervise and teach him such skills as mowing the lawn, watering outdoor plants and flowers, raking and disposing of leaves, and shoveling snow.

While changing a light bulb may seem like a simple skill, you should still supervise your child as he does this for the first time. If he has fine-motor coordination or directionality problems, he may find the task to be a challenge. Caution him not to turn the bulb too tightly, and teach him to look for directions about the maximum wattage that can safely be used in the lighting fixture.

Demonstrate how to make a bed, particularly how to handle the corners of a fitted sheet. Have him follow your demonstration until he can do it on his own. Suggest a schedule for washing the sheets, but keep in mind that this isn't a high priority for most teens.

There's not a lot of glamour in the act of doing laundry, but it's a necessary chore. It can even produce a certain degree of satisfaction. Learning how to manage his laundry will increase your teen's self-esteem and will further ready him for ultimate independence.

In the *New York Times Magazine* article, "It All Comes Out in the Wash," poet and writer Kathleen Norris notes, "Laundry is one of the very few tasks in life that offers instant, gratifying results. It's also democratic; everyone has to do it, or figure out a way to get it done."

Parent tips for helping your teen learn laundry and clothing care

Continue to use think-alouds to demonstrate how to do laundry. Model how to read the care tags on clothing for any special instructions, such as "dry clean only" or "lay flat to dry." Demonstrate how to separate laundry into lights and darks, how to measure and add detergent, and how to load and operate the washing machine and dryer. Explain that laundry wrinkles when it sits for more than a few minutes in the dryer after its cycle, and that hanging and folding right away helps prevent the need to iron. Finally, demonstrate how to remove, sort, and fold (or hang) clean laundry and return it to the appropriate drawer or closet.

Teach your teen how to replace a missing button or mend a simple seam. If he has visual-motor problems, he will benefit from using a threader, available in fabric stores or sewing centers.

Demonstrate how to iron clothing. Start with a flat item, such as a cloth napkin, and gradually advance to shirts. Provide step-by-step instructions about temperature and steam settings. Model how to maneuver the items as you iron them. Supervise your teen as he irons items of increasing complexity until he's comfortable with the iron and can use it safely. Keep in mind that individuals with spatial or visual-motor difficulties may require extended practice in this skill area. Buying wash-and-wear clothing is a great way to minimize this chore.

Take your teen with you to the dry cleaner so he can observe the process of dropping off and picking up items that should not be washed at home. Discuss the associated costs of dry cleaning and the need to budget for this service.

Meal preparation

People need to eat, and no one does this as well as a healthy adolescent! Teens who are preparing for an independent life in the community need to know how to do more than bake chocolate chip cookies—they need to learn how to plan and prepare full meals, a multistep process that many people, even without an LD, find daunting. Planning a balanced and tasty meal requires imagination, a basic understanding of nutrition, the ability to obtain necessary ingredients, and a series of skills that may pose a challenge to your teen with LD. For example, if he has difficulty reading, working with recipes may be hard for him. If he has trouble understanding written or spoken language, common meal planning terms such as "appetizer" or "main course" may be unfamiliar. If math is an area of weakness, he may become frustrated when he has to adjust recipe ingredients according to the number of people for whom he's planning to cook.

Parent tips for helping your teen learn to plan a meal

By middle school, start discussing the meals you eat—note the mix of protein, vegetables, and carbs on the plate. Talk about the foods your child enjoys, their nutritional value, and begin to discuss how to build a balanced meal.

Help your teen plan cooking projects by buying one of the many cookbooks written for kids that provide easy-to-read-and-follow recipes. As he grows more comfortable with the format of cookbooks, introduce him to more sophisticated versions.

While teaching your child to plan meals, try to model your decision-making via more think-alouds. Be sure to mention any ancillary needs (e.g., "Since we're having burgers, we'll need to put out ketchup and mustard when we set the table."). Thinking aloud about each step of the meal planning and preparation process will help your child learn aspects of the process that may seem obvious to you.

When helping your teen plan his first meals, note exactly when each part should be prepared and cooked. Creating a chart that outlines the entire process eliminates the need for on-the-spot decision-making, which can be very stressful for any new cook, particularly someone with LD.

Once a meal is planned, the next step is to make sure the necessary supplies are on hand. Unfortunately, a grocery store is a chaotic environment, and navigating the aisles and checkout line can be very stressful and overwhelming. Characteristics of LD add to this challenge. Teens who have difficulty reading may struggle with aisle signs and food labels. Those with math problems may find they have trouble calculating the cost of sale items. People with visual memory problems often can't remember the layout of the store and as a consequence, wander the aisles looking for particular items. Those with visual figure-ground discrimination problems may find it especially difficult to locate the specific brand of bread or cereal they want among the dozens of choices on the shelves.

Parent tips for helping your teen learn to shop for groceries

Begin by pointing out the categories of foods and the layout of the aisles at the grocery store, noting, for example, that breads are grouped together and that spaghetti and sauce and other food items commonly used together are placed in close proximity. When he's ready, divide up the grocery list and have him pick up several items on his own.

Explain unit pricing and how you make decisions about purchases with unit prices in mind (e.g., "The big box of this cereal costs more but is cheaper by unit. We eat a lot of this, so it won't have a chance to get stale. I'll save in the long run by spending a little more now.").

Encourage your teen to use a calculator to keep track of the accumulating cost of the food being placed in the cart. Explain that, particularly for those working within a budget, tracking purchases when shopping is a very important routine.

Point out the differences among the various checkout lines. Explain the etiquette of the express lane (e.g., "Be sure you have only up to the number of items the sign permits.").

Explain and model how to use coupons and store membership or discount cards to save money.

> *I gave my daughter the responsibility of going through the market sales ads from three different markets each week. With her coupons she matches up what is on sale with the ads. So she saves in two different ways. She saves our family from $100—$400 each month. She also is in charge of restaurant coupons. We never eat out anymore without getting a bargain. This has been an excellent ego lift for her. She has learned so much.*
>
> "Anniversary Survey." SchwabLearning.org

Cooking presents a challenge for many teens with LD, although most welcome the opportunity to learn, since they are pleasantly rewarded by a tasty snack or meal as a result of their efforts. If, for example, your child has difficulty with written or spoken language, he may need extra help to understand common cooking terms, such as "sauté" or "dice," and may need assistance reading recipes. If he has trouble with fine-motor coordination, he may well find it difficult to peel, slice, and chop. And if he has difficulties with time management, he's at risk of burning or under-cooking food he prepares; showing him how to use a food-timer is invaluable. Work patiently with your child to help him learn to prepare food. Cooking together is a great bonding activity, and your efforts will result in his attaining this key life skill.

Parent tips for helping your teen learn to prepare food

Your young teen should be able to step in as your cooking assistant, performing simple steps such as mixing ingredients, slicing, and measuring. Demonstrate as you explain cooking terms (e.g., "bake" versus "broil") as they are introduced in recipes you prepare together.

Show your teen how to use the various appliances and equipment needed for basic cooking. Introduce one at a time—blender, oven, stovetop, microwave oven, food processor—and let him practice using each until he can do so safely and comfortably, without your coaching. If he has difficulty remembering the steps involved in using an appliance or piece of equipment, write them on an attached Post-it note.

Encourage him to use this written support as long as he needs it.

Explicitly teach your teen how to use kitchen knives. Emphasizing safety, supervise as he practices slicing and chopping until he's comfortable handling and using them for various food preparation functions.

There are tools that will facilitate your child's success in the kitchen. For example, buy a cookbook featuring photographs that show how the recipes will look when they are completed. Color-code measuring spoons and cups, marking the 1/4 teaspoon and 1/4 cup with red nail polish, a red marker, or red tape; the 1/2 teaspoon and 1/2 cup with blue; and so forth. Doing so provides an additional visual clue that will help him differentiate these similar-looking items as he cooks.

As you work with your teen in the kitchen, help him collect his favorite recipes in a file box to take along when he moves out on his own.

Serving a meal—and cleaning up afterward—requires coordination. It entails choosing appropriate serving dishes and utensils, providing any necessary condiments, and socializing. Once the meal is over, the dishes must be cleared and washed, leftovers safely stored, and the table and kitchen cleaned up. Teens with LD may have difficulty with these secondary aspects of meal preparation. Those who have organizational problems may find it hard to decide when and in what order various parts of the meal should be served; those with fine-motor problems may be clumsy and drop food or utensils; those with spatial difficulties may have difficulty washing dishes and thoroughly wiping down the counters and table.

Parent tips for helping your teen wrap up the meal preparation process

Provide guidelines for dealing with leftover food. Discuss how long foods can be safely stored in the refrigerator and how to properly store leftovers in aluminum foil, plastic wrap, or food containers. Demonstrate how to label and date leftovers to be refrigerated.

As foods begin to go bad, show how they look and smell before you throw them out. Although this is an unpleasant strategy, it's the best way to teach this essential information.

Demonstrate how to wipe down the counter, table, and sink. Supervise as your teen practices this important skill until he is thorough enough to ensure that safe standards of hygiene will be maintained in your kitchen (and eventually in his!).

By the time their children are nearing completion of high school, many parents request that they cook one meal per week for the family. This provides an opportunity for practice in the safe and familiar confines of the family kitchen before having to work in a kitchen they have to establish on their own. Help your teen get started by verbally walking through the full meal planning process beforehand and making lists of all steps, from shopping to cooking to setting the table to cleaning up. The need for your supervision will taper off as he becomes more experienced and comfortable with the process of planning and preparing meals.

Money management and consumer skills

Even young children can learn basic money management and consumer skills as they begin making purchases with their savings. By middle school, they are ready to be introduced to more complex skills, such as budgeting their allowance. Teaching your teen money management and consumer skills will help him avoid many of the problems that surface for adults with LD.

A major financial rite of passage for youth with and without disabilities is the establishment of a checking account. Your teen's LD may cause problems as well in this area of money management. For example, he may misspell or invert numbers on checks (e.g., writing *61 or 19* instead of *16*). If his memory is poor, he may not always remember to record his bank transactions (e.g., ATM cash withdrawals) or pay bills on time. If he has spatial issues and misaligns numbers in his check register, he will be more likely to make calculation errors when reconciling his account.

Real-life Math Challenges

Joe has math difficulties that make it hard for him to calculate the cost of a CD on sale at 25 percent off. In addition, he's at times unsure of how much change to expect when he buys a snack at the local convenience store.

Toward the end of high school, teens need to learn how to manage a checkbook and pay bills. Opening a real checking account at a local bank is the best vehicle for learning this skill.

Parent tips for helping your teen learn how to manage a checking account and pay bills

Many individuals with LD prefer carbon checks, which help ensure that all transactions are recorded. After modeling for your teen how to write a check, slip an example into his checkbook to remind him of how it's done. Provide a "crib sheet" with correctly spelled numbers to be stored in his checkbook for easy reference.

People who are comfortable with technology often find budgeting software (e.g., Quicken) and online banking services helpful for managing their money. If your teen has access to his checking and savings accounts online, he can check his transactions and balance (and transfer money) anytime.

Since your teen isn't likely to have many bills to pay while he is still in high school, consider having him use his charge account for personal expenses, such as gifts, to provide an opportunity to develop good bill-paying habits. Help him set up a home office space where he can keep all the items needed for successful money management and bill paying, including:

- **Supplies:** Paper, pens and pencils, tape, a ruler, paper clips, a stapler, stamps, and a calculator.
- **Accordion file:** Important papers may be filed under separate headings, such as "bank statements" or "unpaid bills."
- **Budget book:** To record expenditures and realistically estimate future expenses.

- **Calendar:** Used to note the receipt of monthly bills and to record when each is due (Posthill and Roffman).

When your teen prepares to leave home after high school, assure him that you will continue to be available for support and advice as he puts his new money management skills into practice.

Beyond managing money well, your teen will need to be proficient in consumerism and savvy to consumer scams. Like all teens, he may be vulnerable to impulse buying beyond the limits of his budget. Aside from this typical adolescent issue, there are a variety of ways individuals with LD may get into money-related trouble, often starting as early as their adolescent years.

Learning Responsible Consumerism— The Hard Way

When eighteen-year-old Dick started bouncing checks, he got scared and went to his parents for help. After some investigation, they discovered that he had succumbed to the sales pressure of a local gym, which had pitched a "great deal, available today only" when he had gone in to inquire about membership. He had signed a contract immediately, had written a large check on the spot, and had thrown himself into a negative account balance in his checking account.

Becoming a responsible consumer is essential for successful adjustment to adult life, yet many adults with LD rank handling money and banking as the most difficult among the problems they encounter. By helping your teen learn skills in this area, you will prepare him to enter adulthood as a fiscally responsible individual who is prepared to avoid common financial pitfalls.

Parent tips for helping your teen develop consumer skills

Help your child learn about money by providing an allowance and increasing it to match expanded expenses as he grows older and more responsible. Help him develop short-term and long-term financial goals. Have him start by saving a portion of gifts and earnings for future modest purchases, such as a DVD or article of clothing, and build to saving for an evening out or more expensive items.

Work in partnership with your teen to establish a basic budget early in his adolescent years. Have him list all of his anticipated expenses, including school lunches, entertainment, clothing, and miscellaneous items (e.g., CDs or snacks), and establish a weekly budget to manage his allowance and earnings from any jobs he may have. Many individuals with LD benefit from using a "budget envelopes" book, an inexpensive and handy tool, available in most stationery stores, which has separate envelopes for each specific budget category. If your teen chooses to use this tool, he should place enough cash for his various budget categories in each envelope at the beginning of every week and make a commitment to spending the allotted funds only for the stated purposes. This is a very concrete way to develop the concept of budgeting and is a highly recommended first step in the process of learning how to manage money.

Begin orienting your child to a variety of types of stores. In each, note the groupings of items and explain that, although the layout varies by store, the groupings tend to be consistent. Point out the aisle signs and conduct think-alouds as you shop (e.g., "We need some Band-Aids, so I'm looking for the sign that says which aisle has first aid supplies. If I can't find them there, I can ask the clerk at the customer service counter where they are."). By the end of middle school, your child should be able to find items he commonly uses (e.g., school supplies). By the end of high school, he should be able to shop on his own at any of these stores for basic items.

Help your child learn the sizes of the shoes and clothing he wears. Too many parents of middle and even high school students with LD continue to select their children's clothing well beyond the point when this type of control is appropriate. By middle school, your teen should be able to choose his own clothes (within guidelines you have set). This is one way you can foster the self-determination necessary for successful adjustment to adult life.

Discuss tipping with your child. List the kinds of people commonly tipped (e.g., waiters, bellhops) and how to determine the correct amount for each person based on the quality of service and the going rate. When you dine out together, have your teen calculate the tip using a tip chart (available in most stationery stores) or calculator.

Your teen needs to know about basic contracts, such as rental leases, gym memberships, cell phone agreements, and Internet service contracts. Talk about these, and warn him about high-pressure sales tactics. Encourage him to seek assistance from a family member or trusted friend before signing any contract he doesn't fully understand.

Go over the wise use of credit. Your child's special ed curriculum should have introduced the basics of charge accounts, mortgages, and car loans. Continue discussing at home how credit cards work as well as the associated dangers of using them. When he reaches age eighteen, numerous banks will start sending invitations to apply for credit cards. Choose one reputable bank, and have him apply for a card with a credit limit of $500 or less. Discuss the kinds of items he may charge, and walk him through the process of paying the monthly bills— preferably in full to avoid having to pay interest while still establishing a credit history.

It's crucial that your teen learn how to protect his identity. For example, he needs to understand the importance of shredding financial mail (e.g., the numerous credit card applications he will receive) and related documents before throwing them in the trash. It's important that he learn to whom it is safe to disclose his social security number (e.g., at a doctor's office) and that he is highly vulnerable if he reveals it (or his bank PIN) to the wrong person.

Getting around

Perhaps no one activity more clearly represents independence than being able to travel around on one's own. Sadly, people with learning disabilities often have difficulty in this arena. A variety of LD-related factors may inhibit their ability to travel effectively and efficiently from one location to another. Some of them are likely to affect your teen with LD. Your child is not alone with challenges.

Challenges Associated with LD

Michael has trouble reading and finds it difficult to decipher road signs; as a result, he more often than not ignores them out of frustration. He also has spatial problems, which make following maps a chore, and he subsequently finds it difficult to navigate around new or unfamiliar areas.

Brooke has trouble distinguishing east from west and right from left and, as a result, gets lost with some regularity. She also has problems estimating travel times and frequently arrives late to her destination.

Aisha regularly loses her way. She has weak visual memory, so landmarks are of little help to her. She is good about asking for help when she gets lost, but due to receptive language difficulties, she has trouble understanding the directions people give her; due to weak auditory memory, she finds it difficult to remember the sequence of rights and lefts she should be taking.

The adolescents in the above examples don't let their LD stop them from getting out and about within the community. All have found ways of overcoming the navigational problems that result from their LD. Michael uses MapQuest.com to get step-by-step directions and has learned to ask pedestrians for assistance if he is having difficulty finding his way. Brooke has learned to allow herself an extra cushion of time for travel to important appointments. Aisha has learned to write down all directions people give her.

Your child can also learn how to compensate for his weaknesses. Although there are many complex skills involved in getting around, teens with learning disabilities are able to manage this aspect of independent living if they're given explicit training and support. Your help in this area can make a big difference.

Parent tips for teaching your teen to get around

Practice reading maps with your child. Start by discussing simple routes; gradually make the hypothetical journey more complex. Teach him how to use online mapping tools (such as Yahoomaps.com) that offer maps as well as written directions between any two addresses. Be sure to have him print out the directions both ways, since simply reversing the directions often doesn't work for the second leg of a round trip. When your teen understands how to read a map and use these tools, have him plan a short trip or two, first with your supervision and then on his own.

Teach your teen how to read transportation schedules. If you live in a town with a local bus route, review the schedule together. Point out the Departure and Arrival columns, the weekday versus weekend timetables, and other pertinent information (such as fares, departure and arrival points). If there's a map of the route, suggest marking the way from one location to another with a colored marker. Once it's clear that he understands how to use the schedule, send him on a short trip that will require him to practice his ability to read transit schedules, his newly acquired map-reading skills, and safety tips you've discussed in advance (e.g., keeping his wallet in his front pocket when he's in crowds to safeguard against pickpockets).

☞ Discuss how to estimate the travel time between two places. Many factors (such as traffic or mass transit problems) can cause delays. Encourage him to make a "dry run" for important appointments, such as job interviews, to gauge how much time to set aside for travel on the actual day. Suggest that, like Brooke in the example, he build in at least a ten-minute cushion of time in case of unexpected travel delays.

☞ Teach strategies that will help your teen avoid getting lost. Many people who are prone to disorientation in new places write down simple directions. Use a think-aloud to demonstrate taking note of where you've left the car when you go to a crowded parking lot (e.g., "Okay, we're in row 19, right in line with the main entrance to the mall."). Encourage him to jot this information down.

☞ If your child carries a cell phone, help him program frequently-dialed phone numbers (of family and friends) into his phone's directory. If he finds himself lost or in an emergency situation, he may be nervous, so being able to call for assistance at the touch of a button will be a tremendous help.

☞ When traveling by plane or train, talk through each step of the trip—reading the Departure and Arrival boards, checking in, going through security, and so on—to prepare him for independent travel. If you don't travel regularly, take your teen on a field trip to the airport or train station to learn these important skills.

☞ Model tying a colorful item to the handle of your suitcase when you check your baggage on family trips, and explain that practicing this strategy will make it easier for him to spot his luggage in the baggage claim area when he travels on his own.

☞ Discuss the importance of identifying appropriate resources in a variety of situations. Think-alouds will help him understand your thought process. (For example, you might say, "Okay, we aren't sure where the train station is. There's a policeman; I'll ask him if we're headed in the right direction.") Explain to your teen that we *all* get lost or disoriented at times, and that asking for help is a sign of resourcefulness rather than weakness. If he has memory problems, suggest that he repeat the directions back or, better yet, carry a notepad and pen so he can write down the directions he hears.

☞ Review safe pedestrian habits, particularly if your teen has a problem with depth perception and may not be able to judge the speed of oncoming vehicles. Remind him that it's safest to use crosswalks and obey traffic signals to get from one side of a street to the other.

Special advice for drivers

As I explain in *Meeting the Challenge of Learning Disabilities in Adulthood*, driving presents its own set of challenges.

With all of its complexities, driving can be of particular concern to individuals with LD and ADHD. Difficulties vary and can develop for a multitude of reasons. For example, people may find it difficult to train their right foot to recognize the difference between the accelerator and the brake and, on standard [manual] transmission vehicles, to train their left foot to simultaneously work the clutch. They may find it challenging to develop a working understanding of the reactivity of the steering wheel, which must turn only so much to pass another car but must turn even more when it is time to round a corner. They may struggle to interpret what they are seeing in the rearview mirror. On cars with manual [standard] transmission, they may have difficulty moving from one gear to another, particularly to reverse, which generally requires an additional thrust. Further, they may have considerable difficulty learning how to parallel park. Indeed, many find it difficult to meld the many separate aspects of car handling into one coordinated driving experience (Roffman 2000, 191).

If your child would like to learn to drive but you're afraid that he might not be able to master the necessary skills due to the severity of his LD, contact a hospital rehabilitation center in your area for an assessment. By using simulators to test his reaction time, depth perception, and other related skills, professionals there can determine whether the disability is severe enough to prohibit him from obtaining his license. If he is found to have the potential to become a safe driver but is in need of extra support as he learns, the rehabilitation center should be able to recommend a local driving school attuned to the needs of those who would benefit from special instruction due to disabilities.

Parent tips for helping your teen master driving

☞ If your teen does get a driver's license, help him differentiate right from left by placing R and L Post-it notes on the dashboard as cues. Teach him that there are both low-tech and high-tech ways to keep from getting lost. One high-tech item is a geographical positioning system (GPS), which can direct him to his specific destination. Low-tech strategies include keeping maps, a compass, and a directions file with clear instructions both to and from frequent destinations in the car's glove compartment.

☞ It's critical that he understand the importance of concentrating fully on driving at all times. Talking on cell phones or changing CDs while driving are dangerous risks (and illegal activities in an increasing number of states). Model safe behavior by pulling over when you need to talk on your cell phone or change a CD.

Searching for an apartment

Leaving home is a physical and emotional milestone, the culmination of the transition process for most teens after they have developed self-determination and the requisite independent living skills. If your child has made independent living his goal and he's mastered all of the skills he needs to maintain a household, he may be ready to start looking for an apartment after leaving high school. Although his life skills curriculum should include units on apartment living and the apartment search process, these lessons are all the more effective when parents can supplement them with discussions at home.

Parent tips for helping your teen prepare for the apartment search process

 Discuss the financial and social pros and cons of living with roommates.

 Practice reading real estate listings in the newspaper and on the Internet. Help your child decipher abbreviations (e.g., "ww" = wall-to-wall carpets; "EIK" = eat-in kitchen) and key concepts (e.g., first and last month's rent, security deposits).

 Talk with your teen about the importance of location when he is seeking a place to live. Discuss the value of safety, proximity to public transportation and/or availability of parking, and nearness of convenience stores.

 Cover the basics of leases, landlords, and utilities that may not be included in the monthly rent bill.

 Once your child has moved into his new place, help him organize his personal world. For example, guide him as he establishes set places for belongings such as his keys, cell phone, and eyeglasses. Encourage him to use open shelving and, if needed, to label drawers clearly.

If things are put away, they're gone for me. I have to have everything out, where I can see it. I use milk crates for storage—I swear by that as a system.

Personal interview with Kate, a young adult with LD

Health and medical needs

A critically important step in preparing for independent adulthood is learning to take care of one's own health and medical needs. You and your teen will need to discuss exactly what his needs are so he can prepare to monitor them with increasing independence. Once again, aspects of his learning disability may affect his ability to function in this area.

- If he has a *poor memory*, he is likely to have difficulty remembering details of his medical history, including surgeries he's had and medications he takes.

- If he has a *receptive language problem*, he may become confused by doctors' explanations of diagnoses and prescribed courses of treatment.

- If he has an *expressive language problem*, he may have trouble explaining his symptoms and/or conveying his medical history.

- If his *reading is weak*, he will probably have difficulty with medication labels and the directions on medical equipment (e.g., a heating pad).

- If *writing is an area of weakness*, he will find it a challenge to fill out forms at doctors' offices.

- If *math is an area of challenge*, it may be difficult for him to measure liquid medicines and calculate the time intervals for taking medications.

- If he has *poor visual discrimination*, he could have problems discriminating between pills and pill bottles that look alike.

There are a number of practical suggestions that will ease his difficulties. You can help your teen with LD develop an understanding of his medical needs, of how to convey his needs to others, and how to take medications safely.

Parent tips for teaching your teen healthy medical habits

Discuss routine health care, such as the need for annual physicals and twice-yearly dental appointments.

Teach your teen basic medical vocabulary, such as the names of key specialists (e.g., gynecologist, orthopedist) and terms for common symptoms (e.g., muscle spasm).

Discuss the symptoms of common ailments, such as a cold or migraine headache, and the appropriate treatments (including medication) for each. Show him how to use a thermometer, and discuss how to treat a fever.

Explain the purpose of hospital emergency rooms, and discuss circumstances that would warrant calling 911. Review common illnesses and injuries (e.g., a sprained ankle) that would not require an ambulance but might require a visit to the ER.

By late high school, it's time for your teen to start scheduling his own medical and dental appointments. Coach him regarding the information he will need to have handy (e.g., any changes in address, phone number, insurance carrier), remind him to have his calendar available, and stay with him the first few times he takes on this responsibility. If possible, have the office mail any forms to him ahead of time, and help him complete them prior to the appointment. This will save him from having to fill out the forms on his own—under pressure—in the waiting room.

Before you take your teen to the doctor, help him write up a list of symptoms and questions to present to the physician. Advise him to continue to do this once he starts going to appointments on his own. Many people find it helpful to take a tape recorder to appointments to record and later review any discussion of symptoms, diagnoses, or treatments. Encourage him to consider this practice when he starts going to medical appointments by himself.

Compile a personal medical fact sheet for your child. In list form, write out his personal medical history (including surgeries), your family's medical history, any prescription or over-the-counter medications he takes as well as any medication allergies. Have him become familiar with his health history, and let him practice referring to the fact sheet for answers. Help him update it as needed.

Encourage your teen to disclose his learning or attention problems to his health care providers and self-advocate for any needed accommodations (e.g., jotting down the treatment plan for him if he has weak auditory memory).

Managing medication is an essential skill for independent adults. Your teen will not be ready for independent life until he can manage his own medications.

Parent tips for helping your teen manage medications

 Model how to consult with a pharmacist. Point out that pharmacists are available to advise patients regarding correct dosages of new medications and possible side effects to watch for, and to help create a schedule of exact times when pills should be taken. If you know of a particularly good pharmacist (one who takes the time to listen patiently and who provides clear, accurate instructions), recommend that your son fill his prescriptions with him or her.

 Encourage your teen to enlist trustworthy family members or friends to help him read and understand medicine labels and directions. Remind him of the importance of reading about each new medicine before taking it.

Show your child how to measure liquid medications (e.g., cough syrup) using a hollow-stem medicine measuring spoon, available at drug stores.

Demonstrate how to mark similar-looking medicine bottles with brightly colored tape so your child can readily tell one from the other.

Show your teen how to use technology (e.g., his wristwatch or cell phone) to cue him to take his next dose of medicine.

Leisure activities

Most parents recognize that their teens with LD need extra support to learn how to manage their physical health. Yet many fail to realize that their children would also benefit from help in learning how to plan and pursue leisure activities that *contribute* to good health, *foster a sense of wellness,* and *bring balance* to their lives.

Too few parents are aware of the many ways the characteristics of LD can affect leisure skills. Visual perception difficulties, for example, have implications for a variety of recreational activities. If your teen has a deficit in this area, he may have trouble catching, batting, or kicking a ball; he may find it difficult to catch onto dance steps; he may have problems tracking the ball or puck in spectator sports; he may even have a hard time finding his seat again after going for refreshments in a theater or sports stadium.

Teens with LD often are aware of what they like to do but don't know how to translate interest into activity, or how to find others with whom they might engage in their preferred leisure pursuits. If they are to have the quality of life we all wish for our children, it's important for them to identify their strengths and interests and to find satisfying ways to pursue them. Discuss the questions in Figure 1 with your teen to help him think about how he would like to make use of the leisure time he has.

FIGURE 1

Helping Your Teen Think about His Free Time

Discuss the answers to these questions with your teen.

✓ What kinds of things do you like to do for fun? How often do you do them? What keeps you from doing them more often than you do?

✓ How much money per week can you afford to spend on leisure activities?

✓ What kinds of individual activities have you enjoyed in the past (e.g., working out, playing computer games)?

✓ What kinds of *individual* activities would you like to try out now or in the future?

✓ What kinds of *group* activities have you enjoyed in the past (e.g., singing in chorus in school, bowling, drama club)?

✓ What kinds of group activities would you like to try now or in the future?

✓ Are there opportunities nearby to try out these new activities?

✓ What's preventing you from trying new activities? Can you travel independently to the activities that interest you? If not, how might you arrange for transportation?

✓ What help from others do you need to make it possible to try out these new interests?

Help your teen identify satisfying individual and group leisure pursuits as well as venues within the community where he can access them. Throughout middle school and into high school, children's interests are likely to be in sports and activities sponsored by the school or local clubs. As your teen matures, try to help him identify how he can continue to pursue his interests within the larger community. Investigate membership at the local YMCA or at nearby gyms for physical activity. Look into the offerings at area centers for adult education or arts centers. Your place of worship may have a chorus that could fill your teen's interest in music. If he's a hiker, check the membership requirements of such affinity groups as the Sierra Club. If he's an avid reader, check whether the local library sponsors a book club for community members. If your teen plans to attend college, help him investigate recreational/interest pursuits on campus. At first, provide assistance as he works to build his preferred leisure activities into his life; later, fade your help and just provide moral or financial support as needed.

Parent tips for teaching your teen leisure time skills

Teach your teen how to use and take care of leisure equipment, such as exercise machines and video games.

Explore volunteer and community service activities (e.g., the local food pantry or animal shelter) in your area, and discuss whether volunteer work interests him. If so, consider going with him the first time or two to help him understand what's being asked of volunteers.

☞ Teach your teen how to work around his weaknesses and compensate for any difficulties that interfere with his leisure activities. For example,

- If he has trouble visually recalling dance steps he has seen, encourage him to talk through the actual movements, step-by-step, to provide auditory input that will help him recall where his feet should go.

- If he has difficulty finding his seat at the stadium after he goes for refreshments, advise him to look for visual markers and jot them down on a pad of paper to help him avoid getting lost.

- If he worries about not being able to sit still during a performance, suggest that he squeeze a squishy-ball to expend some energy while he stays seated.

- If he has difficulty reading the menu when he's out to eat with friends, suggest that he be the last one to order and choose what someone else has already selected. If there are restaurants he frequents regularly, he can take a menu home and read it there, with your assistance if needed.

☞ Help your teen create a master monthly calendar to clearly schedule his routine tasks, including school, work, chores, and extracurricular activities. Have him add non-routine activities, such as medical appointments, and note that empty space on the calendar represents free time. Young adults with LD benefit from this level of structure, which provides a visual sense of tasks and of free time for leisure pursuits.

SUMMARY

Studies suggest that adolescents with LD remain dependent on their parents longer than their non-LD peers. Through life skills courses and assistance from their parents, they can develop the skills they will need when they do venture into independent living. Chapter 3 outlined specific topics covered in the transition planning process. Instruction in key community living skills may focus on grooming and personal hygiene, housekeeping, meal preparation, consumerism and money management, and leisure time activities—all depending on the individual needs of your teen with LD.

CHAPTER 5

POSTSECONDARY LEARNING: NEW CHALLENGES AND OPPORTUNITIES

by Loring C. Brinckerhoff, PhD

It's crucial that you and the rest of your teen's IEP transition planning team believe in your child's potential to continue learning at some level after high school—and that you convey the message that lifelong learning is a realistic goal. The key is to find the right match of learning opportunities to fit her interests, aptitudes, and personal objectives.

WHY CONTINUE LEARNING BEYOND HIGH SCHOOL?

Jobs increasingly require an education beyond high school. In fact, an individual's earning capacity rises directly in proportion to the level of education achieved.

Earnings estimates for full-time, year-round workers, over forty years

On average, persons possessing a bachelor's degree would earn $2.1 million, which is approximately one third more earnings than can be made by workers who did not complete their college education, and nearly twice as much as workers who have only a high school diploma. Individuals who have earned a master's degree have earnings estimates of $2.5 million, and a doctoral or other professional degree holder is expected to reach $4.4 million or higher.

"The Value of Higher Education." **EducationAtlas.com**

A growing number of students with learning disabilities realize that in order to be better prepared for the world of work, graduating from high school is essential, and post-secondary learning is highly desirable.

Despite substantial benefits—not only with regard to potential earnings but also in terms of enhancement of social status and personal growth—far too few students with LD continue their learning beyond high school, largely because they are not encouraged, assisted, [or] prepared to do so (NJCLD, 1994). Results from the National Longitudinal Transition Study-2 suggest that fewer than 60 percent of parents expect their child with LD to graduate from high school with a regular diploma. Low expectations are a powerful impediment to personal growth; for this reason, it is critically important that parents of youth with LD raise their expectations. Research suggests that students whose parents have higher expectations for postsecondary outcomes have higher grades and basic skills levels than do students whose parents have lower expectations for postsecondary participation.

> *Today, as I reflect on my experience growing up with a learning disability, I realize what an important role my mother's advocacy played in shaping my own self-advocacy skills as a college student. Because of her guidance, I learned how to believe in myself and be a stronger person—to articulate what I needed to succeed in school. Having a parent who believed in me when others didn't made all the difference for me growing up. My mother was and is my strongest champion and advocate.*
>
> Dana P., Wheaton College student, message board post from the National Center for Learning Disabilities. NCLD.org

THE SPECTRUM OF POSTSECONDARY LEARNING OPPORTUNITIES

The path to continued learning after high school can and will be distinctly your child's own. It may consist of study at two- or four-year colleges, vocational-technological schools, non-degree transition-focused programs, or adult education centers. The hope is that you and your teen will search for (and find) the best postsecondary option for her.

Non-degree transition programming

There are a handful of campus-based life-skills-oriented transition programs for highly motivated students with severe learning disabilities who function in the low–average range intellectually. Although most of the students who enroll in such programs would be too challenged by the academic requirements of a degree program, they are nonetheless very interested in experiencing college life, continuing to learn, and preparing for independent adulthood. Courses are very practical and often community-based, focusing on vocational training, development of daily living skills (e.g., cooking, shopping, cleaning, money management), and social skills training. Many offer continued transition support as graduates move from the campus into apartments and jobs.

> I never thought I'd be able to go to college like my older sisters, but then we found the Threshold program, and it was perfect for me. I majored in early childhood and prepared for the day care assistant teacher job I've held ever since. I also learned to cook and how to manage my money and a lot of other independent living skills before I moved into the apartment I live in now, but the best part was making a lot of friends. I'd never had that before, and the friendships I made have lasted since graduation.
>
> Alumna of Threshold, a non-degree program at Lesley University

In addition, there are transition programs that primarily center on independent living. Participants in these programs typically live in apartments with supervision and work locally as they develop the daily living skills to assume more independence. Some programs in this model maintain collaborative relationships with nearby community colleges, where participants may study if they choose to do so.

Two-year colleges

The majority of students with learning disabilities who enroll in postsecondary education start by spending a year or two at their local community college. Many worry that, because they have low GPAs, missing pieces in a college-prep curriculum, or weak scores on the ACT or SAT, more competitive options are out of reach. They gravitate toward community colleges, which have an open admissions policy, meaning a high school diploma or a GED is all that is necessary for admission.

Although a community college may not have the same status as a big-name state university or a select private college, it is a very good option for many students with and without learning disabilities. Class size tends to be smaller in community colleges than at large universities, tuition is relatively low, and a wide range of vocational, remedial, and developmental courses are offered (students generally take a placement examination to determine at which level to begin their college course work). Students may take a few courses in areas of interest, a series of vocational courses to train for particular employment, or pursue an associate's degree with the intention of later transferring to a four-year institution. Given that the program of study for an associate's degree is typically only two years in length, students have quicker access to employment and more flexibility to plan a schedule that may better meet their needs.

In addition to the financial and academic advantages of the community college option, it is a popular route for psychological reasons as well—since, as a non-residential institution where all enrolled are commuters, it allows students to "try out" the college experience close to home, near family and friends.

Another alternative for those who wish to pursue an associate's degree is attending a private two-year junior college. Because a two-year junior college tends to charge lower tuition rates than a typical four-year university, a junior college shares the community college's appeal of being economical and offering a high-quality education, but is often more selective in its admissions process.

As technology advances and distance learning becomes more commonplace, online associate's degree programs are gaining popularity. Online learning is a particularly appealing option for students who already have strong computer skills and need a flexible class schedule to fit around home or work responsibilities.

> For more information about online degree programs, visit **PrincetonReview.com.**

Technical training

Some students with LD elect to pursue careers in technical areas that de-emphasize reading and writing skills and instead stress hands-on experience. Tech-prep programs often involve a partnership between secondary vocational technical schools and community colleges. If your child is clearly directed toward a career in mathematics, science, or engineering, a technical college curriculum may be a more appropriate choice for her.

Some students meet success in college settings that offer a co-op curriculum, which focuses on a combination of course work and work experience, rather than in institutions with more traditional liberal arts curricula.

Four-year colleges

Four-year colleges and universities are largely residential, require students to matriculate and pursue a degree, and charge considerably more than community colleges for tuition, room, board and fees. The 2006 average is $12,000 a year for public institutions and $29,000 for private institutions, but at many the costs run even higher. Although some have open enrollment policies, many are selective, requiring solid scores on standardized admissions tests such as the ACT or SAT, rigorous academic preparation in high school, a strong grade point average and class ranking, and excellent recommendations. Some highly selective colleges require a personal interview and/or submission of an art portfolio for certain programs.

Keep in mind that four-year settings come in all shapes and sizes ranging from rural colleges with 400 students to large university systems with tens of thousands enrolled. Large universities typically offer the broadest range of educational, athletic, and social experiences. Public universities are known for providing a high-quality education at a reduced cost to in-state residents. Liberal arts colleges often appeal to students who are looking for a smaller college environment and a broader liberal arts curriculum.

LEGAL CONTEXT FOR POSTSECONDARY STUDY

The laws that apply before and after your teen exits high school

It's very important that both you and your teen understand that IDEA does not apply to higher education. Colleges do not offer "special education"; they are not required to design special programs for students with disabilities and are not legally mandated to provide individual aides or tutors. Colleges instead provide "disability services." Under Section 504 of the Vocational Rehabilitation Act of 1973 and the Americans with Disabilities Act of 1990, discrimination based on disability is prohibited. "Otherwise qualified" students with disabilities (students who have equivalent qualifications to non-disabled applicants) must have equal access—through the provision of reasonable accommodations or auxiliary aids—to the full range of educational programs and activities offered to all students on campus.

Decisions regarding specific accommodations to be provided are made on an individual basis. The college may select the aid or services it will provide, so long as it is effective. For example, if a student asks Disability Services (DS) to provide a laptop computer and special note-taking software, the DS office may instead offer as a reasonable accommodation to pay another student in each of her classes to be her note-taker.

> *Section 504 and the ADA are civil rights mandates designed to ensure access; they are not special education laws.*
> Joseph W. Madaus "Helping Students with Learning Disabilities Navigate the College Transition Maze." *Teaching Exceptional Children*, Jan/Feb 2005: 32.

Disability laws ensure access, but students must still meet the university's standards for admissions, course content, and graduation; these standards do not have to be altered for students with disabilities. Moreover, students are only protected if they self-identify and provide documentation of their disability. If a student chooses not to self-identify and struggles academically, there is no retroactive protection, so those who think they might need help should disclose early and take advantage of services and accommodations offered by the school.

One new college student who was struggling came to me not too long ago and told me she had always had support services in the past but wanted a "clean slate" when she went on to university. She felt after all those years of services, that maybe she was "all better." I'm afraid this was wishful thinking on her part. LD doesn't go away, though the symptoms may decrease in certain arenas. Certainly if a student has needed assistance with writing in the past, this is going to be an area where support is likely to be needed in postsecondary learning.

Dr. Arlyn Roffman. "LD Talk: Transition to Post-School Life." NCLD.org

The transition process and planning postsecondary learning

As discussed in Chapter 3 on transition planning, both you and your teen are full members of the IEP transition planning team under IDEA. She has an opportunity to shape her own destiny by participating in the development of her annual goals and selection of her high school classes. Her IEP becomes her passport to accommodations, modifications, and special services under the law, and describes in detail what she needs in order to participate fully in the classroom and on district-mandated testing. Unfortunately, as noted earlier, many high school students comment that they have not been included in their IEP decision-making process and complain that their parents have "set everything up" for them. In the guise of protecting students with LD from failure and stress, too many well-meaning parents and high school personnel fail to elicit student perspectives—and ultimately keep them from practicing self-determination.

Be sure your teen's IEP includes goals that help her develop learning strategies, organization, time management, problem-solving, and social skills that will be needed in a post-secondary setting.

> *As an adult with a learning disability who was able to succeed in college, I can sincerely say it takes a lot of personal sacrifices to do well. There were many weekend nights when I stayed in my room instead of going to a party. Exams that took my friends two hours to study for took me four or five hours. I had to have all my papers completed five days before they were due so I could find someone to proofread them.*
> Jason P. Kaplan. "Sometimes College Should Wait." (18).

The self-determination skills practiced in your child's transition planning IEP meetings will serve her well in college, where she will have to self-disclose and self-advocate for needed accommodations in her classes. As the IEP transition planning team works to develop goals related to post-secondary learning, the focus should be on your teen's need to:

- Develop the self-awareness discussed earlier in this book. She must understand her own learning style and be closely familiar with her academic and personal strengths and weaknesses. She needs to know how she learns best, be aware of the circumstances under which she does not learn well (e.g., in noisy environments; in a classroom where the teacher lectures without providing any visuals), and be familiar with the compensatory learning strategies, accommodations, and modifications that make it possible for her to succeed in a classroom.

- Cultivate the social skills and self-advocacy skills to enable her to meet her social and academic needs in college (e.g., approaching the Disability Services office on campus to describe her disability and request the accommodations she needs).

- Understand that while there are no IEPs in college, the documentation that enabled her to qualify for services under IDEA in high school may allow her to access needed accommodations in college.

- Know her legal rights and responsibilities (e.g., to self-identify and provide documentation) with regard to postsecondary learning, specifically in terms of accessing accommodations.

Parent tips for preparing teens to think about postsecondary education during the IEP process

Prepare your teen for the IEP transition planning process by encouraging her to talk about the various options for her future. Remind her that continuing to learn is a viable choice, and make sure she selects high school classes that will keep post-graduation options open.

Encourage her to participate actively in planning her postsecondary future. This may entail bringing to her IEP meeting a list of high school courses she wants to take or a list of potential colleges she is interested in visiting.

☞ Check whether it is the norm in your school district to invite a postsecondary education representative to the IEP transition planning meeting to discuss the realities of the college experience and help set appropriate goals for postsecondary learning.

PREPARING FOR COLLEGE IN HIGH SCHOOL

The road to college starts well before your child turns eighteen. It's very much to her advantage to start preparing both emotionally and academically early in her high school career.

Choosing courses to prepare for college

If attending college is your teen's objective, avoid allowing her to be locked into a general studies curriculum. Too often, high school freshmen with LD are counseled to take "modified" or simplified courses that earn academic credit toward graduation but provide only limited training and background knowledge for transition to postsecondary education and employment. If your child thinks she may want to attend college, it is important that she not be scheduled for resource room assistance during the periods when essential college-preparatory courses are held. Students who fail to select certain college prep courses, such as algebra or chemistry, during their freshman or sophomore years of high school may find themselves less qualified for admission and woefully underprepared for the rigors of a college curriculum.

College admissions counselors read the high school transcripts of applicants for evidence of successful completion of a wide array of courses (science, history, literature, foreign language, art, math, music). Since they carefully consider the quality of high school courses, if your teen is college-bound, she should take as rigorous a course load as she can handle. Her guidance counselor should advise her against taking more than one or two basic courses (e.g., "Nutrition Today" or "Basic Math") per semester. It may look impressive to some that she has earned all A's on her report card; but if she has done so by taking an excess of basic courses and electives, her record will do little to impress college admission personnel, who routinely recalculate high school GPAs based on college preparatory course work. It is better for your teen to take a mainstreamed college-preparatory class and earn a C-plus than enroll in a basic course and earn an A. On the other hand, high school students with learning disabilities should steer away from advanced placement (AP) or honors classes if those courses will demand a disproportionate amount of their study time or inordinately pull down their overall high school GPA.

A rule of thumb: If your child can earn a respectable grade of B or above in an accelerated class, it could help to support her application to a competitive college by further indicating that she is otherwise qualified (according to the ADA), despite the learning disability.

Junior year course work is perhaps the most critical, as it will allow your teen to lay the final ground work for her postsecondary experience. By her third year in high school, you and the IEP team should review her transcript carefully to be sure it reflects the quality of course work necessary for entrance to college. If it does not meet that standard, then the program of study should be upgraded and adjusted accordingly. Her academic program should be selected with considerable thought, given that college admissions officers look very carefully for any changes or trends in the educational rigors in a student's program of study. Depending on her postsecondary goals, she should be warned that if she elects to take only two or three college-preparatory classes per semester, she may not appear to be prepared for the rigors of a college curriculum that typically consists of four or five courses per semester. Guidance counselors should address these issues early on with her to be sure that she understands the ramifications of her choices.

A word of caution about waivers: Whenever possible, waivers from mathematics or foreign language classes should be avoided in high school because they may prohibit access to certain undergraduate programs at which such proficiencies may be required despite the presence of a disability. A waiver should only be granted in high school after your teen has made a "good-faith effort" at passing the class with resource support. In addition, her diagnostic testing should substantiate the need for the course waiver (e.g., waiving a foreign language based on severe language-based learning disabilities with related processing or memory deficits).

Understanding the differences between high school and college

As your teen attempts to make an informed decision regarding whether to pursue higher education, it is important that she be forewarned about some of the differences between high school and college. Although all college freshmen have to adapt to the many differences and encounter new challenges, entering students with LD often face unique additional hurdles related to their disability. First and foremost, they must be aware that after graduating from high school, they lose the entitlement to services afforded under IDEA. As described earlier, under Section 504 and the ADA, they must self-identify and self-advocate for needed services at the postsecondary level.

The bulleted list below (drawn from "Differences in High School and College Requirements" in Brinckerhoff, McGuire, and Shaw, 2002: 30) lists additional significant differences between high school and college. Discuss these with your teen, and consider together how her LD may come into play as she continues her education.

- **In-class time and teacher contact:** Two of the biggest differences that young adults face concerning the move from high school to college are the amount of in-class time and opportunities for direct teacher contact. High school students are in class approximately six hours a day, and it is not unusual for them to have contact with their teachers four or five times a week. In contrast, college classes often meet only once or twice a week, and there are fewer opportunities for faculty-student contact. In addition, college faculty members often have limited office hours; this makes it even more difficult for students to find time to interact with their professors. (With the advent of online courses and e-mail, this is changing somewhat, but the problem remains that students' direct access may only be to a teaching assistant and not to the actual instructor of the course.)

- **Class and classroom size:** Class size is another important variable, given that some college classes may be as large as 200 to 300 students, in contrast to high school classes, which typically have no more than 25 students. During their freshman and sophomore years of college, students are routinely herded into large, impersonal auditoriums with tiny desks for core courses such as "Introduction to Western Civilization." At some large universities, students may only be able to view the professor on a closed-circuit television monitor. Although colleges may consider these settings to be efficient for the broad dissemination of information, such environments provide less-than-optimal learning environments for students who are easily distracted or have organizational problems.

- **Facilities:** Most high schools are a single building or a tight cluster of buildings; college campuses are often vastly different, with dozens of buildings and offices spread over acres. Students with spatial or temporal difficulties may have difficulty finding their way to classes or allocating adequate time to travel across campus to arrive when class begins.

- **Homework:** Typically, students in high school work on assignments at home, but often have the opportunity to complete them in a study hall or during resource room time, if they are in special education. In contrast, college students must learn how to budget study time independently. As a general rule, for every hour of class time, college students need to spend three to four hours of out-of-class time per day preparing their assignments. For students with LD, this rule of thumb should be doubled, given the time needed for rewriting lecture notes, reading, listening to audio textbooks, or integrating course materials from a variety of sources (e.g., texts, class lectures, or library assignments). Taking notes alone can be a very labor-intensive, time-consuming task.

- **Feedback:** Another contrasting point related to assignments concerns the amount and frequency of direct teacher feedback students receive on their work. In high school, homework is often assigned on a day-to-day basis, and students are expected to turn it in daily or weekly for feedback. In college, "homework" often consists of long-range assignments, such as term papers or cooperative projects with peers. College professors seldom monitor students' daily work. In order to become independent, self-sufficient learners in preparation for college, high school students would be well advised to seek out teachers during their junior and senior years who will gradually wean them from day-to-day monitoring of their work.

- **Grading:** It is not unusual for college students to receive only two or three grades per semester. Instead of being graded at the end of a chapter or unit, college students may only receive a grade once a month or following the mid-term and final examinations. For high school students, who are accustomed to receiving more regular feedback from teachers, this often requires an adjustment. High school teachers have been known to grade students based on subjective factors, such as "effort" or "degree of improvement," college faculty tend to be more objective, and the teaching assistants grading work for them are often trained to mark off for all but prescribed responses. As a result, students may find themselves receiving significantly lower grades than they did in high school.

- **Teaching style:** Along with differences in grading systems, the teaching style of college faculty is distinct from those who teach secondary school. High school teachers often focus on teaching factual content; college instructors tend to expect students to think more analytically and synthesize abstract information on their own and integrate course information from a variety of sources, rather than merely parrot back isolated facts.

- **Requirement of self-reliance:** Secondary school teachers often provide external reinforcement of students' work without ever helping them develop the capacity to evaluate their own progress. As a result, many students with LD exit high school without the ability to monitor their work, reflect on its quality, predict academic outcomes, or flexibly adapt their approach to varying academic tasks. High school students with learning disabilities often become overly dependent on teachers and parents, who regularly "rescue" them right up to the finish line before exams or when term papers are due; although most college campuses have a disability services office, few have the personnel to provide drop-in hours for last-minute term paper editing, test preparation, or content tutoring.

- **Personal life:** Perhaps the biggest challenge that your teen will face when she goes away to college is balancing her personal life with academic demands. The novelty of being on a college campus and adjusting to all of the factors discussed above make it particularly difficult for students with LD to stay focused. The free time of high school students is often structured by limitations set by their parents, their teachers, and other responsible adults. On the other hand, college environments require teens to function independently by managing their own time and organizing their days and nights. Students are faced with the freedom to make their own decisions about scheduling time, choosing their own classes and majors, and conducting their social lives. They are often ill-prepared and overwhelmed as they try to strike a balance between their course work and busy social lives.

SAT and ACT preparation

If your child is planning on applying to college, she will need to consider taking either the SAT or the ACT. Every year, about two million high school students take SAT exams, and almost as many take the ACTs. (Since the format of the SAT was changed, the number of students who take the ACT—or who take the SAT and the ACT—has grown.) During the fall of your teenager's junior year (as early as late sophomore year, if requested), she may take the PSAT in order to prepare for the SAT, which focuses on verbal, mathematical, and writing skills.

The SAT Subject Tests are subject-specific examinations in areas such as foreign languages, world history, and biology. Many colleges require one or more subject tests in addition to the SAT or ACT and consider them for admissions and course placement. Your child should review the catalogs and Internet sites of schools of interest to her to find out whether they require SAT Subject Test scores for admission. It will be to her advantage to take Subject Tests just after she completes the relevant courses, while the material is still fresh in her mind.

Your teen's guidance counselor should help her register for the PSAT or the PLAN, which is the equivalent warm-up examination for the ACT. If her documentation supports the need to take these tests with accommodations based on the nature and severity of her disability, her counselor and special education teachers should encourage her do so. Testing accommodations may include a reader, a writer, a taped version, large type, large-block answer sheets, extended time, use of a private room, or multiple test days.

The College Board requires that any accommodation request in excess of 100 percent additional time, or any request for multiple-day testing be accompanied by a copy of the student's IEP or 504 Plan. The school psychologist or the private diagnostician who wrote the report should be sure that the disability documentation is complete and be prepared to provide written verification of the need for alternative testing arrangements. The College Board also has a process whereby the student's high school can supplement older testing with teacher observations on the student's use of accommodations in the classroom.

The College Board has adopted a set of documentation guidelines prepared by Educational Testing Service (ETS) that provide guidance to parents, consumers, and educational testing professionals about the type of documentation necessary to verify accommodation requests for test takers with learning disabilities or attention deficit disorders. Documentation policy statements for ETS can be found at ETS.org/disability.

If your teen anticipates taking the SAT or ACT with accommodations, she should contact her guidance counselor before January 1 of her junior year. Unlike the SAT, the ACT does not routinely send admissions officers all of the scores from previous test administrations. Test takers may select to have only the best scores sent to colleges.

If all of this sounds terrifying, it may be reassuring for students who are not good test takers—whether or not they have LD—to learn that there are increasing numbers of postsecondary institutions that do not require SAT or ACT scores at all. FairTest (FairTest.org) provides a list of more than 700 colleges and universities that do not require SAT or ACT scores for admission.

LEVELS OF LD SUPPORTS AVAILABLE ON COLLEGE CAMPUSES

Campus support services for students with LD vary greatly from one institution to the next, running the gamut from very basic services to comprehensive programming. This is one more reason why it is especially important for you and your teen to do your homework when investigating a particular college.

Basic services

Under the Americans with Disabilities Act, each college and university is legally required to offer a minimal level of support to students with disabilities at no cost and to provide reasonable accommodations, such as textbooks in audio format, course substitutions, reduced course load, and notetakers. Campuses offering the most basic level of services are ensuring equal education opportunities for disabled students and are upholding their legal obligation—though their services may not be extensive enough for your child with LD. Their disability contact person typically wears multiple hats (he or she may also be an attorney, counselor, or nurse on campus) and generally has only limited training in disability matters. Fortunately, an increasing number of colleges are recognizing the complexity of the role of disability officer and are committing more resources to their students with disabilities, hiring at least one knowledgeable individual to serve as the designated point person for all disability matters.

Comprehensive LD programs

Comprehensive LD programs that go beyond the legally mandated services have more personnel in support roles. Typically, the director or coordinator has expertise in learning disabilities and oversees a staff of several full-time professionals and part-time tutors. In addition to basic accommodations, these campus disability support offices may:

- Train faculty and staff to raise awareness about disabilities.

- Offer a wide range of tutorial supports, with subject matter tutoring provided by graduate students, professional tutors, and trained peer tutors.

- Provide individualized academic advising.

- Monitor the progress and adjustment of students with LD.

- Offer in-house diagnostic testing.

- Offer a summer transition program for incoming freshmen or a special one-day orientation before registration.

- Offer additional support in the areas of career planning, learning strategies, self-advocacy, stress management, practical computer skills, test taking, time management, and writing skills in collaboration with on-campus and off-campus services.

- Provide an extensive website, including written policies and procedures regarding course substitutions, LD accommodations, and documentation requirements.

For students seeking support beyond the mandated services, an additional fee of $1,600 to $3,900 applies, depending on the level of service desired. Newer innovations in these settings include peer coaching, tutorials on the use of technology, and technology lending libraries for students. Because of the specialized nature of the services provided, comprehensive LD programs may limit the number of "slots" for students with learning disabilities and may require special application fees.

If your teen is independent, can self-advocate, knows what accommodations are effective for her, and already has a repertoire of strategies to compensate for her LD, she may do very well in a postsecondary setting that offers only limited services. On the other hand, if she requires more structure or is not knowledgeable about her LD or about how to seek help, she would be well-advised to seek a college with a more comprehensive LD program.

THE COLLEGE SEARCH

It is not unusual for high school juniors or even seniors with LD to have little sense of either what they want in a postsecondary setting or of the level of LD support services they need. Most benefit from guidance on how to find a suitable postsecondary program, one with the range of support services that will be compatible with their specific needs, interests, and abilities. The good news is that there are many options available to students with learning disabilities who would like to attend college in the United States and Canada. For instance, the most recent edition of *K&W Guide to Colleges for Students with Learning Disabilities* (Kravets and Wax, 2007) profiles more than 300 institutions with services for students with learning disabilities.

Your teen's guidance counselor or school librarian should teach her how to use college resource guides, directories, and the latest computer-guided software to assist in the college search process.

Parent tips for launching an effective college search

The Couselor-O-Matic tool on **PrincetonReview.com** allows prospective college applicants to search for colleges based on type, region, intercollegiate sports, major, tuition, financial aid, and other factors. Your teen can then use hot links to go from these search results to the home pages of schools to get more information, to compare and contrast school offerings, and even to apply online.

Finding the "right match" between the LD student's characteristics, the postsecondary setting, and the LD support services offered is a time-consuming but critically important process. Planning should focus on matching your teen's interests and abilities with the most appropriate postsecondary setting. Based on their own personal visits to many institutions, guidance personnel can be especially helpful in describing the diverse range of two- and four-year options available to students after graduation. Unfortunately, high school guidance counselors often have a caseload of several hundred students and have limited time for individual mentoring through the college selection and application process. It is essential for you and your teen to work as closely with her counselor as time allows to determine if the type of LD services offered at the colleges of interest to her will be a good fit, given her aptitudes and needs.

If her counselor's time and advice seem to be inadequate, you may want to consider hiring an outside consultant who can assist you and your teen with the college search process. Independent consultants visit many colleges each year and are able to keep up with specifics, not only about their various programs, but also about personnel, policies, documentation requirements, and even the culture of the campus. Their services range from hourly consultation about choosing a school to a full package that takes a student through the process of selecting appropriate options, preparing for the SAT/ACT, filling out the application, preparing essays, practicing for the interview, even coaching about what to wear for the visit to campus. Naturally, fees range considerably for these services, not only based on specifics contracted for, but also based on where in the United States you live—fees tend to be higher on the coasts.

More information about private college counseling is available at the website for Independent Educational Consultants Association (IECA), IECAonline.com, and at the site for National Association of College Admissions Counselors (NACAC), NACAC.com.

Parent tips for launching a successful college search

☞ It's a good idea to start with a list of prospective schools—at first *without* regard to disability-related concerns—based on what your child wants (not necessarily on what *you* want), academic programs offered, admissions-related requirements, costs, financial aid, location, community resources, athletics, and social activities.

☞ Only after this short list is created should you bring disability-related concerns back into the equation, urging your teen to refine her selections by becoming familiar with the LD services provided at each listed institution. By comparison shopping, you can work together to find the best match.

☞ Pay careful attention to the admissions criteria, which often vary widely from one institution to the next. Generally speaking, look at minimum entry requirements based on high school class rank, grade point averages, prerequisite course work, and SAT or ACT scores. In addition to these factors, if your child is able to meet the minimum standards for admission, she may want to consider the academic qualifications of the "average student" for a given institution. By gathering this information, she may start to eliminate those colleges that appear to be too competitive or that do not provide an array of generic student support services.

☞ If this process becomes too emotionally charged in your family, consider hiring a college consultant. If financial constraints prohibit doing so, it may be helpful for your teen to speak with a trusted adult friend who has been through the process and can step in as a back-up informal advisor.

☞ College selection is complex and stressful. The process begins in eighth grade and concludes with high school graduation. Following a timetable provides structure to what often feels like an overwhelming process to many students with LD and their families as they weigh their many options for continued learning. Figure 1, "Timetable for Transition Planning for Students with Learning Disabilities and ADHD" (Brinckerhoff, McGuire, and Shaw, 2002 38–42), will help you and your teen ensure that she is on track to achieve her postsecondary goals. Look over the timetable with your teen. Note that some of the steps listed are discrete and time-sensitive (e.g., applying for the SAT with accommodations); others are meant to be taken care of at some point in the high school experience, but not necessarily at a particular grade level (e.g., writing an IEP goal). The timetable will help your teen view the postsecondary planning process as a series of coordinated steps over a period of years involving input from a number of supporting players. It will engage her in taking increasing responsibility for her own learning outcomes and will help you gradually transfer control and responsibility to her and begin to prepare yourself for her launch into adult life.

☞ Once she develops a list of schools she would like to learn more about, your teen should make a point of seeking out their college admissions representatives at "LD College Nights," which are often held locally or regionally. Meetings with regional representatives from two- and four-year colleges at high school college fairs provide an opportunity to discuss admissions requirements, curricular and recreational options, and the range of disability services available on campus.

A Timetable for Transition Planning for Students with LD or ADHD

Grade 8: Preparing for High School Success

Students with learning disabilities or ADHD need to:

- Take the most academically challenging program in the most integrated setting possible.
- Consult LD teachers as needed on how to become independent learners.
- Actively participate in IEP meetings and suggest goals that focus on study skills, time management, and test-taking strategies.
- Seek opportunities that will foster self-determination and independence through increased responsibility at home and in school.
- Develop money management skills and assist in meal preparation, shopping duties, and caring for clothing.
- Expand academic interests through electives and extracurricular activities.
- Begin to identify preferences and interests.
- Keep a calendar for activities and homework assignments.
- Develop appropriate social skills and interpersonal communication skills.
- Learn about high school expectations and offerings.

GRADES 9 AND 10: TRANSITION PLANNING BEGINS

Students with learning disabilities or ADHD need to:

- Continue to practice Grade 8 goals.
- Learn what learning disabilities are and are not.
- Develop an understanding of the nature of their own disability and learning style.
- Clarify the exact nature of their learning disability or ADHD by reviewing the diagnostic report with an LD specialist or psychologist.
- Learn about civil rights and the responsibilities of high schools and colleges under IDEA, Section 504, and the ADA.
- Self-advocate with parents, teachers, and peers.
- With parent input, select classes (e.g., word processing, public speaking, study skills) that will prepare them academically for college or vocational/technical school.
- Avoid temptation to "retreat" to lower-track classes, if college-bound. Select solid college prep courses.
- Be wary of course waivers and carefully consider implications of those choices.
- Use LD support and accommodations in math or foreign-language classes rather than seeking a waiver, if possible.
- Seek classroom teachers and learning environments that are supportive.
- Enroll in remediation classes, if necessary.

- Focus on "strategy-based" learning with LD teacher.
- Balance class schedules by not taking too many difficult courses in the same semester, or too many classes that play into the areas of weakness.
- Beware of peer advice on which classes to take and avoid.
- Provide input on who should participate in the planning team.
- Become a co-leader of the transition planning team at the IEP meeting.
- Demonstrate independence by writing some of their own IEP goals.
- Try out accommodations and auxiliary aids (e.g., taped textbooks from Recording For the Blind & Dyslexic [RFB&D], note-takers, laptop computers, extra time on exams) in high school classes that are deemed appropriate by LD teachers.
- Know how, when, and where to discuss and request needed accommodations.
- Learn about technological aids such as talking calculators, four-track tape recorders, optical scanners, handheld spell checkers, voice-activated software, and electronic day planners.
- Know how to access information from a large library.
- Meet with a guidance counselor to discuss PSAT registration for October administration (in Grade 10).
- Arrange with guidance counselor to take PSAT/ PLAN with accommodations if warranted.
- Register for SAT Subject Tests, if appropriate.

- Use "score choice" option for SAT Subject Tests, to release only those scores desired.

- Gain a realistic assessment of potential for college and vocational school.

- Consider working at a part-time summer job or volunteer position.

GRADE 11: TRANSITION PLANNING IN THE JUNIOR YEAR

Students with learning disabilities or ADHD need to:
- Continue to practice Grade 8, 9, and 10 goals.

- Review IEP for any changes or modifications for the upcoming year.

- Advocate for a complete psychoeducational evaluation to be conducted by the beginning of Grade 12 as an IEP goal.

- Present a positive self-image by stressing their strengths, while understanding the influence of their learning disability.

- Keep grades up. Admissions staff look for upward grade trends.

- Arrange for PSATs with accommodations in mid-October. Apply for a social security number if necessary.

- Match vocational interests and academic abilities with appropriate postsecondary or vocational options.

- Explore advantages and disadvantages of community colleges, vocational technical schools, and four-year colleges, given the learning disability and/or ADHD.

- Meet with local Department of Rehabilitation Services (DRS) counselor to determine their eligibility for services. If eligible, ask counselor for assistance in vocational assessment, job placement, and/or postsecondary education or training.
- Consult several of the popular LD college guides and meet with a college advisor to discuss realistic choices.
- Finalize arrangements for the SATs or ACTs with necessary accommodations. Visit the website for ACT (www.ACT.org) and College Board (www. CollegeBoard.org).
- Start with a list of fifteen to twenty colleges based on the LD guides, visit the websites for these institutions, and request specific information about LD services offered.
- When reviewing a prospective college website, determine how available support services are on campus. Is there specific information on the site about disabilities?
- Preview colleges with CollegeBound.net or http://USnews.com search site.
- Narrow listing to eight to ten preliminary choices based on competitiveness, location, curriculum, costs, level of LD support, etc.
- Request any additional information needed from college (e.g., applications to LD program, specific fee information, financial aid forms, etc.).
- Discuss with parents, counselor, regular education teachers, and LD teachers the anticipated level of LD support needed in a postsecondary setting.

- Understand the differences between an "LD program" and support services models.

- Attend "LD college nights" at local area high schools. Assume responsibility for asking questions of college representatives.

- Develop a "Personal Transition File" with parent and teacher assistance. Contents should include: current diagnostic testing, IEPs, grades, letters of recommendation, and student activity chart or resume.

- Narrow options to five or six schools ranging in competitiveness and levels of LD support.

- Prepare a "College Interview Preparation Form" to use during the campus interviews.

- Arrange for campus visit and interviews in advance. Don't just drop in on the LD support services office staff and expect an interview.

- Consider sitting in on a class or arrange to meet college students with learning disabilities through the support services office. Listen to their firsthand experiences.

- Meet with the designated LD services coordinator to determine the level of support offered and to assess the nature of the services offered (e.g., remedial, compensatory, learning strategies, etc.).

- Determine how important self-advocacy is on campus. Determine how accommodations are arranged with faculty.

- Follow up with a personal thank-you note to the disability coordinator.

- Consider a private LD preparatory school or a "13th year" program if postsecondary education doesn't seem to be a viable option.

- Consider enrolling in a summer orientation program specifically for students with learning disabilities or ADHD. Contact HEATH Resource Center (800-54-HEATH) for more information.
- Apply for a summer job, volunteer position, or career-related work experience.

GRADE 12: TRANSITION PLANNING IN THE SENIOR YEAR

Students with learning disabilities or ADHD need to:
- Continue to practice Grades 8, 9, 10, and 11 goals.
- Update IEP quarterly.
- Retake the SATs or ACTs to improve scores. Note that scores may be flagged as "special" or "nonstandard." Discuss implications with guidance counselor.
- Select several colleges as "safe bets" for admission, several "reasonable reaches" and one or two "long shots."
- Consider early decision only if convinced that a particular school is the best match.
- Note all application deadlines. Complete a paper-based application to use as a model for on line versions.
- Consider downloading applications or using the Common Application.
- Be alert to early application deadlines for some LD college programs.

- View a variety of college shopping networks: CollegeNet (www.CollegeNet.com); CollegeLink (www.CollegeLink.com); AppZap (www. CollegeView.com/appzap).

- Carefully select people to write letters of recommendation. Give teachers and counselors plenty of time. Pick a teacher who knows their personality. Recognize that such letters may include comments about the learning disability. Keep a Personal Transition File.

- Keep a listing of names, phone numbers, and addresses of postsecondary contact people and copies of all applications in their Personal Transition File.

- Role-play the college interview with guidance counselors or special education teachers.

- Decide whether to disclose their learning disability or ADHD prior to admission.

- View "Transitions to Postsecondary Learning" video and complete student handbook exercises with LD teachers (Eaton/Coull Learning Group, 800-933-4063).

- Pick up all necessary financial aid forms (FAF) for college from guidance counselor. Males who are eighteen years old must register for the draft to be eligible for federal aid forms.

- Discuss financial considerations with guidance counselors and search the Web using FinAid.org or http://fastweb.com.

- Tap into Department of Rehabilitation Services. If eligible for job guidance, consider enrolling in internships or job-shadowing experiences that permit "hands-on" skill building.

- Formulate a realistic career plan.
- Forward mid-year grades to colleges.
- Wait for the news from colleges. If the news is good, then:
  - o Rank postsecondary choices based upon their ability to successfully compete and the provision of support services to meet their unique learning needs.
  - o Notify all schools of their decision.
  - o Pay housing deposit by May 1, if appropriate.
  - o Arrange to have final transcript sent to the college.
  - o Hold an exit interview with guidance counselor and LD teachers.
- If the news is not good, then:
  - o Appeal the admissions decision, especially if some new "LD-relevant data" were not considered or overlooked.
  - o Pursue any of a variety of alternatives such as applying to a less competitive college with a "rolling admissions" policy; enrolling in a postgraduate year at an LD preparatory school; enrolling in a community college with academic support services.
  - o Consider taking a college course for credit over the summer at a community college or in conjunction with a summer orientation program.

From *Promoting Postsecondary Education for Students with Learning Disabilities* by L. Brinckerhoff, 2002, Austin, TX: PRO-ED, Inc. Reprinted with Permission. Originally adapted from "Making the Transition to Higher Education: Opportunities for Student Empowerment," by L. C. Brinckerhoff, 1996, *Journal of Learning Disabilities*, 29: 135–136. Adapted with permission.

> For many students with learning disabilities, discussions with campus representatives can be a real eye-opener, as they realize that few community colleges and relatively few four-year institutions offer the same comprehensive array of special education services that are available in high schools.

Try to make it possible for your child to visit the campuses of the schools of greatest interest to her. If you and she can't manage to visit in person, review some websites that offer "virtual tours" of the campus. This may not be as exciting as being there and stopping off at the campus bookstore to buy a sweatshirt, but it may help give you both a feel for the school. Consult: PrincetonReview.com; CollegeView.com; WiredCollege.com; and CampusTour.com.

If a campus visit is possible, encourage your teen to call and arrange for an interview with the director or coordinator of LD support services to see if the LD services will be adequate to meet her needs. (Note that this may be in addition to the standard applicant interview. At the former, she should ask questions related to LD support services—such as those listed below—and at the latter, she should tout her academic and extracurricular accomplishments.) Most disability service providers prefer to interview a prospective student alone, without parent prompting, in order to get an accurate reading of her level of motivation, social skills, and understanding of her disability. During the interview, your teen should seize the opportunity to address any "irregularities" in her academic history, such as low ACT or SAT scores despite a strong high school GPA, or lack of participation in extracurricular activities due to outside tutoring or work demands. She should generate a list of well-thought-out questions regarding the college's curricular offerings, admissions process, required disability documentation, available accommodations, and especially the level of learning disability support services offered on that campus.

Barr et al. (1998, 1–3) suggest the following questions as particularly helpful for prospective students who are learning to sort out college options for themselves:

- For how many students with learning disabilities does the campus currently provide services?

- What types of accommodations are typically provided to students with learning disabilities on campus?

- Will this college provide the specific accommodations that I need?

- What records or documentation of a learning disability are necessary in order to arrange for academic accommodations for admitted students?

- How does the college protect the confidentiality of the records of applicants and enrolled students?

- How is information related to the documentation of a learning disability reviewed?

- Does the college have someone available who is trained in and understands the needs of adults with learning disabilities?

- What academic and personal characteristics have been found to be important for students with learning disabilities to succeed in this college?

- How many students with learning disabilities have graduated in the past three years?

- Are there additional fees for learning disabilities-related services and, if so, which services are considered beyond the scope of Section 504 and the ADA?

> If your teen has qualifications that look marginal on paper but is able to convey her potential and abilities orally, the campus visit and interview will be especially important for her. Be prepared that the typical campus interview does not involve parents. You may be asked to sit patiently in a red leather chair in the waiting room and review glossy college viewbooks while your child has her interview!

After visiting the campus, you and your teen should debrief about the overall campus environment. What did you learn about the social and learning climate of that particular postsecondary setting? How is the housing? What did she learn about financial aid? How did she feel about the location? Did the level of disabilities services seem adequate to meet her needs?

Urge your teen to write a thank-you note to the interviewer. This brief handwritten note (not an e-mail) should come from her, not you, if it is to make a positive impression on the admissions officer.

Once your teen has narrowed down her choices, help her organize for the intense application process ahead.

Parent tips for beginning the application process

☞ Help her develop a system for organizing the catalogues that have been filling your mailbox all year so that she can weed out all but those of particular interest.

☞ Since different schools are likely to have different due dates, help her note each application deadline on a calendar.

☞ Encourage her to make use of her Transition Planning Portfolio (TPP), which will be particularly helpful as she begins the college application process. Often developed at school as an IEP goal, as an independent study project, or as part of a summer transition program between junior and senior years of high school, the TPP is a personal file of all transition-related documents, for eventual use in application to college or employment. She may maintain her portfolio in the traditional paper-and pencil format in a file box or accordion file, as an "e-portfolio" (a series of electronic file folders), or on a personal website; the key is for her to have files or sections that organize materials needed in the transition process.

• One section should contain school records: copies of past and present IEPs, high school transcripts, and a one-page summary of extracurricular activities.

• One section should contain her disability documentation, including her most recent psychoeducational evaluation with specific diagnostic information; a listing of all approved accommodations from high school; and a copy of her ACT and/or SAT scores.

- One section could contain college-specific information, questions to ask during the admissions interview, an extra copy of a completed Common Application form, an updated resume, a personal essay describing her learning disability, and nonconfidential letters of recommendation.
- Other sections dedicated to employment will be further described in Chapter 6 on work.

☞ One of the keys to success for students with learning disabilities is to be able to articulate what their disability is all about, how it affects their day-to-day functioning, and how they have learned to compensate for it. In order to field questions about her disability, encourage your teen to draft a brief one- or two-paragraph essay about her LD to include in her Transition Planning Portfolio, which could subsequently be folded into an admissions essay or included as an application addendum.

☞ As a prospective student, your teen should be encouraged to arrange to meet other college students with learning disabilities who have used the support services on campus and sit in on a class so she can develop a realistic view of college life.

APPLYING TO COLLEGE

Senior year often commences in a flurry of college-application activity, with students filling out numerous applications and writing college essays. For students with LD, the process is largely the same, but they need to consider the "double match" factor—the postsecondary institution and the level of

LD support available on campus—in their application decision-making equations. There are several specific issues that should be considered.

Should she apply early?

More and more, prospective students are opting to apply early decision or early action. If your teen knows exactly what she wants in a college and feels passionate about a particular school, she may want to consider applying early because, in general, colleges admit a higher proportion of students as early applicants than from the normal pool. The admissions landscape is shifting with regard to early decision, and some highly selective universities are dropping this option. Check the most recent policies of any college to which your teen is considering applying early.

A word about the difference between early decision and early action: the former is usually binding (i.e., if your child is admitted, she is bound to attend); the latter is not binding. While early decision offers the prospect of more security, it may limit your financial aid options—and it also requires that you and your child make a definitive decision earlier in the process. If admitted via early action, your child may elect to accept, but she will be under no obligation to attend that institution. She will be able to bank this admission and still apply to other colleges during the regular admissions cycle. If she applies early decision, she must pledge that, if accepted, she will attend that school. Her guidance counselor must also attest that she will attend the institution, if admitted.

If your teen chooses to apply early, in most cases she must submit her application by November 1 of her senior year. Typically, she will hear within six to eight weeks.

Should she use the Common Application ("Common App") or other similar approaches to apply?

Applicants with LD should be encouraged to use the "Common App" form, which is available online at CommonApp.org. Most applicants choose to submit the form electronically. According to the Common Application website, this standard form is honored by 300-plus member colleges nationwide. Students may also apply online via PrincetonReview.com. A similarly time-saving approach is to connect with the CollegeLink program, a fee-based service that allows applicants to complete a single application on their personal computer, which can be forwarded to about 500-plus institutional subscribers. CollegeNet.org provides a similar service, and for a small fee your teen can print out and apply electronically using the application form from more than 1,500 colleges.

Should she disclose her LD?

It is important that students with learning disabilities learn how to strategically market themselves in the admissions process. Perhaps the biggest issue to consider is whether it is advisable to disclose their disability when they apply. Your teen is under no legal obligation to disclose that she has a disability; under the ADA and 504, disclosure is entirely optional.

Disclosure is a very personal and individual decision. If the college has a well-defined LD support program, it is likely that disclosing the disability will do nothing to detract from the application, and in some cases it might even enhance a student's chances of acceptance. If the college or university downplays the fact that it has LD support services, then it may be prudent for a student to avoid mentioning the disability in her application.

There are circumstances under which disclosure may be warranted in either case. For example, if your teen did not take or complete a core foreign language or math requirement in high school, she should address this point in a personal statement or addendum. She should think carefully about how to present her strengths and challenges during the application process; it is very important that she discuss with you and her counselor how to word this disclosure statement. Whenever possible, it is advisable to put a positive spin on her learning disability and on her accompanying strengths. If she does choose to reveal her disability, she should tie the disclosure to her documentation (e.g., auditory processing disorder, attention deficit) and present a rationale as to why certain requirements have not been met or why certain grades were lower than anticipated.

Who should write her letters of recommendation?

Your teen should use great care in selecting the people who will act as her personal references. Letters of recommendation from family, friends, clergy, and elementary school teachers who are unfamiliar with her current educational strengths carry little weight in the application process. (Even letters from the teachers she had as a first-year high school student are considered less valuable than those from teachers who've had her in class more recently.) Admissions officers generally frown on ploys such as letters from "connected" people, who often lack a substantive personal connection with the applicant. A letter of recommendation from a general education teacher in one of her college preparatory classes who reports that your child is ready for the challenges of college despite her LD is likely to capture the attention of the admissions committee, more so than a routine letter from a guidance counselor who barely knows her. If she chooses to self-identify as having a learning disability, then a letter from the LD resource room teacher might be appropriate if it substantiates her level of motivation and achievement potential for college level work. Letters from special education teachers can shed valuable light on her prospects for success in college if they realistically highlight her abilities and address her level of motivation to succeed in school.

How can she best market herself?

Applicants need to be reminded that the high school transcript is the number-one credential that establishes their potential for college success. Your child's best marketing strategy is, of course, to do as well as possible in her high school classes. That said, there are strategies specific to the application process itself that may help her.

Caution your teen not to send more information than is requested and to avoid exaggerating her achievements—a thick file does not necessarily impress admissions staff. Her application should reflect dedicated extracurricular involvement, but it is important for her to know that colleges are far more impressed by a student's intense involvement in one or two extracurricular activities than in many that have clearly only been pursued casually.

The essay is a golden opportunity for your young adult to spotlight an aspect of her life or to discuss a significant personal struggle, a family experience, or an intellectual pursuit that reaches beyond the conventional high school curriculum. It is best if she writes about a topic that is personally exciting to her rather than about a subject that "sounds intellectual" or that will come across as less than genuine and sincere. Urge her to highlight some of her unique abilities, such as superior math skills, sports talents, acting flair, or leadership. If your teen does choose to self-disclose, writing about her learning disability and how she has effectively compensated for it can be a very good topic if it is handled in a creative and self-affirming manner. When a student's application is in question or is considered "borderline" by admissions personnel, disclosure of the disability may well serve to strengthen her case if she can show that she has overcome her deficits. However, she should be aware that disclosure of her LD could work against her in the admissions process at some schools.

> College admissions officers are savvy enough to identify essays that have been written by someone other than the applicant. Provide lots of encouragement and help her proofread—but do let her write her own essay.

In your teen's essays, she should also mention why each particular college is the right match for her, given its reputation, location, offerings related to her career interests, and level of available LD support services. She should specifically note anything that impressed her on the campus tour and visit, during her interview, or on the school's website.

Many colleges now require electronic applications, but if your teen has to fill in a paper application, advise her to make a draft copy first and then produce a final version in ink to send out. Work with her to proofread all materials she plans to submit to avoid mechanical errors that will make a poor impression. She should ask her high school guidance counselor to review all application materials for completeness at least two or three weeks prior to the application deadline. If she does not receive a postcard from a school confirming receipt within three weeks of sending her application, it is wise to contact the admissions office to verify its safe arrival.

Helping your teen find her way into higher education is a collaborative process. As her parent, you can assist your teen by having high expectations, validating her dreams, and nurturing her social development and academic growth. Secondary school personnel can help prepare her for the challenges she will encounter by beginning to replicate some of the demands of postsecondary education while she is still in high school. A postsecondary disability service provider can help by joining the IEP transition planning team and collaborating to present the higher education experience realistically and develop goals that will enable her to enter college after graduation. The key collaborator, of course, is your child. She is the one who must develop self-understanding, self-awareness, and self-advocacy. She is the one who must master the critical study skills, learning strategies, social skills, and daily living skills that will enable her to continue her education successfully.

Financial aid considerations

While the average cost of college has gone up annually at a rate twice the rate of inflation over the past decade, financial aid has also increased substantially in recent years. On the average, full-time students at private institutions receive about $9,600 in aid in the form of grants and tax benefits, and there is more than $122 billion in financial aid available for college-bound students. Your child will need to apply for financial aid early in the spring of her senior year, using the

Free Application for Federal Student Aid (commonly known as FAFSA), which is required by all private and public schools (fafsa.edu.gov). Some organizations may offer additional scholarship funds specifically for students with learning disabilities. The Anne Ford Scholarship, available through the National Center for Learning Disabilities at http://ncld.org/awards/afscholar-info.cfm, is one such award. PrincetonReview.com, Fastweb.com, and CollegeBoard.com allow you to search a vast array of scholarship offerings. The HEATH Resource Center's "Financial Aid for Students with Disabilities" is another helpful resource.

Useful Websites about Transitioning to College

Getting Ready for College: Advising High School Students with Learning Disabilities heath.gwu.edu./PDFs/GR.pdf

Transition to College: Strategic Planning to Ensure Success for Students with Learning Disabilities LD.org

Teens with LD and/or ADHD: Shopping for College Options SchwabLearning.org/teens

Going to College: Successful Transitions for Students with LD
NCLD.org/index.php?option=content&task=view&id=898

IF COLLEGE IS NOT THE PATH . . .

Many students with LD are not ready to continue learning immediately after exiting high school. Some lack the motivation to move on to higher education; some are unprepared to contend with the academic demands or the social pressures of postsecondary settings; some fear the emotional costs of entering a new learning environment after exiting high school.

While up to 20 percent of high school graduates with LD do go on to college, nearly half of them leave before receiving a degree. Talk candidly with your teen about her dreams for her life after high school. Delve into her concerns, and weigh the pros and cons together to determine whether college is a suitable goal after she finishes high school. For some, taking time to work or travel is a better option than college, at least in the short run, as it allows students to mature and develop a better sense of the interests they may wish to pursue at the postsecondary level. If your teen isn't ready for the plunge into full-time studies, she may choose to take individual classes or attend community college part-time, just to get her feet wet with little pressure.

Watching peers make exciting plans for the future that don't reflect the plans of your child can be painful for the entire family. The experience can be particularly difficult in today's ultra-competitive environment of super-achieving kids.
Melinda Sacks. "When Your Teenager's Peers Are Headed to College, but He is Not." SchwabLearning.org/teens

Students who are not college-bound often feel awkward and stressed during the period of time when peers are taking PSATs and SATs, going on college tours, filling out applications, asking teachers for letters of recommendation, hearing whether they've been admitted, and deciding which colleges they will attend.

Parent tips for helping your child cope with an alternative postsecondary path

If your teen is not planning on continuing her education after high school, provide support and encouragement for making alternative plans, such as working or traveling.

It's bound to happen—a well-meaning neighbor, family member, or friend will ask, "So where do you want to go to college?"... Having an answer in mind ahead of time can help those not heading to college avoid feeling embarrassed or put on the spot. Here are some perfectly reasonable answers that work for many kids.

- I'm taking some time off after high school to figure out what I want to do.

- I'm going to take some classes at the local junior college.

- I'm looking into alternatives, and I'm not sure yet.

Melinda Sacks. "When Your Teenager's Peers Are Headed to College, but He is Not." SchwabLearning.org/teens

Help her script a few answers to questions related to post-graduation plans.

 Make sure your teen's transition planning process focuses on vocational and community living goals.

Try to find others who have entered adulthood and have "made it" without attending college who can serve as role models.

Encourage her to conduct an Internet search for "Alternatives to College" to access a variety of sites that will help her consider her options, which include community service programs, leadership training programs, and apprenticeships. Examples of websites for non-college postsecondary options include:

- **Alternatives to College:** Time Out: Internships, Service, Work
  http://nths.newtrier.k12.il.us/services/postHS/alternatives.html

- **The Princeton Review:** Is a Career or Technical Program Right for You?
  www.PrincetonReview.com/cte/articles/plan/cteright.asp

- **Oracle Education Foundation After-High Alternatives:** After High Come Explore the World of Life After High School
  http://library.thinkquest.org/C005172/

Whether or not your teen is interested in pursuing higher education after high school, encourage her to consider some sort of continuation of her learning, even single classes in adult education. Let her know that supports are available in nearly every learning setting and that with a bit of investigation, she should be able to find a postsecondary path that fits her interests, skill level, career path, and budget. Encourage her to view learning as a lifelong commitment with the potential to be both interesting and satisfying despite her learning challenges.

Summary

Now is an exciting time for high school students with LD to be considering their postsecondary options. For many, attending college is an important and realistic goal; for others, pursuing other postsecondary options makes more sense. For those who are college-bound, however, there is a great deal of information to consider and steps to take in preparation for application completion and ultimate enrollment. This chapter provides parents with practical information to support their teenager in this multi-year process of planning for and applying to college. Despite the complexities of the process, your teen should not be discouraged; instead, she should be advised to use the transition planning experience as an opportunity to understand herself better and to explore the array of postsecondary choices available after graduation.

CHAPTER 6
THE PATH TO EMPLOYMENT

THE PATH TO EMPLOYMENT

The path to employment began long ago, when your child first began developing an awareness of community jobs and played at being a firefighter, teacher, or police officer. It continued as he started doing simple chores within your home and began developing a work ethic. It further unfolded as he learned about good grooming and the importance of making a positive impression on others.

Now that he is in high school, he is ready to embark upon the rigorous vocational planning process. As he is exposed to new information about careers during the formal process of transition planning, he will be swept into a period of exploration and evaluation and will begin to determine the shape of his future in the world of work.

Why emphasize work?

Getting a job is a major milestone in adolescent development; it marks increased participation in society and serves as an entrance into adulthood. With it comes increased financial independence and the opportunity to establish a personal identity recognized by the outside world. More than 80 percent of students with LD enter the workforce immediately after high school (Gerber "Starting Out Right"). And even those students with LD who pursue postsecondary learning do so with the goal of eventually becoming employed; schools can help meet the needs of all adolescents with LD when they include preparation for successful entry into employment in the transition planning process.

Obstacles associated with LD

Stepping into employment is an exciting yet anxiety-provoking rite of passage for all youth—especially for those with LD, whose disability characteristics threaten to surface and present added challenges in the workplace. If your child has had difficulty reading during his school years, for example, it would not be unusual for him to experience difficulty at work wading through e-mails, memos, manuals, and other job-related texts. Those who have had writing problems in classroom settings may find it difficult to fill out job applications and compose reports, memos, and the myriad other kinds of written communication required in the positions they may hold. If math has been an area of deficit for your child, he could have difficulty calculating his pay, making change, or performing other on-the-job tasks that call upon ability in this area.

Yet it is the non-academic characteristics of LD—problems in processing, reasoning, communication, coordination, social skills, and attending to tasks—that generally prove to be the biggest impediments to obtaining and maintaining employment. Language processing deficits can cause employees with LD to misunderstand important directions; memory problems may lead to forgotten meetings; disorganization may result in losing items of importance to their work; and weakness in the area of social skills may keep them from being hired, earning the trust and respect of coworkers, or advancing in a job.

Far too many adults with LD are unemployed or underemployed—working at low-level positions, at low salaries, with few benefits. Thus, the need to address this area early and in depth is particularly urgent. Despite the potential obstacles to work adjustment, with good training and guidance your teen should be able to find a position in which he can work around his weaknesses—with the aid of accommodations and modifications, if necessary—capitalize on his strengths and find his place in the work world.

> Among the out-of-school secondary school youth with LD being followed in the NLTS2 Longitudinal-Transition-Study, 88 percent had been employed in the past two years [at least part-time] at a mean hourly wage of $8.14.
> NLTS2 Self-Perceptions Survey, 2006

As a parent, you can do a great deal to maximize your teen's potential for employment success. This chapter will describe the process of career development, introduce available supports, and offer suggestions of how you and his school can foster growth toward vocational readiness.

Parent tips for fostering career success

First and foremost, expect your child to graduate from high school with a regular diploma and have a career—your high expectations are important to his future success!

The more you know about the work world, the better prepared you'll be to support your child as he begins to transition into employment. Try to learn about the job market and specific requirements of various positions so you'll be better able to advise your teen about possible avenues to take.

LEGAL ENTITLEMENTS AND PROTECTIONS

As mentioned earlier in this book, when your teen exits high school, he leaves behind the legal entitlements provided under the Individuals with Disability Education Act. The systems that have nurtured and protected him under IDEA no longer apply, and the people who have been available to meet his disability-related needs will no longer be available. This is a harsh reality; he must understand that when he enters the adult world, he will be left to his own devices to contend with this invisible disability.

It is crucial that parents and teens with LD be aware of the laws that provide civil rights protection for individuals with disabilities. Both Section 504 of the Vocational Rehabilitation Act of 1973 (Section 504) and Title I of the Americans with Disabilities Act of 1990 (ADA) have the potential to affect your child's vocational future. Both are designed to protect him from discrimination based on his disability in all aspects of employment, including recruitment, application, hiring, promotion, transfer, layoff, termination, and leaves.

Section 504

Section 504 of the Rehabilitation Act of 1973 (which applies to employers who receive federal funding of any sort) states that "no qualified individual with a disability in the United States shall be excluded from, denied the benefits of, or be subjected to discrimination under" any program or activity that receives federal financial assistance. Qualified individuals with disabilities must be able to meet the normal and essential eligibility requirements of the position for which they are hired and, with reasonable accommodations, perform the essential functions of the job.

"Section 504 Overview." NCLD.org

Title I of the ADA

Title I of the ADA requires employers with fifteen or more employees to provide qualified individuals with disabilities an equal opportunity to benefit from the full range of employment-related options available to others. People with LD qualify under the ADA, since their disability "substantially limits one or more major life activities"—in this case, work. The ADA prohibits discrimination in recruitment, hiring, promotions, training, pay, social activities, and other privileges of employment. It restricts questions that can be asked about an applicant's disability before a job offer is made, and it requires that employers make reasonable accommodations unless such accommodations result in undue hardship.

It is good news indeed that learning disabilities fall under the protection of these laws and that your child need never be the victim of employment discrimination due to his disability. It is important, however, to be aware that there are some restrictions to this protection.

- Your teen must be *otherwise qualified* for any position he seeks, meaning he must have the ability, skills, and education to perform the *essential functions* of a job, either with or without reasonable accommodations. The essential functions are the minimum required duties and abilities necessary to perform the tasks of the job for which he has been hired. If he is unable to perform the essential functions of the job, it is not considered discrimination if he is not hired.

- An employer is not required to provide *reasonable accommodations*—changes or adjustments that make it possible for an otherwise qualified employee with a disability to perform the duties or tasks required—unless the employee self-discloses his disability and provides verifying documentation. Thus, if your child is unable to perform adequately on the job without an accommodation, he should disclose that he has a learning disability and self-advocate for the specific accommodation he needs in order to perform the tasks required. Legally, he may not be discriminated against based on his need for reasonable accommodations.

- The employer is required to provide accommodations unless doing so would create an *undue hardship*, either by creating an excessive financial burden or by interfering with the nature or operation of the business.

- If he does *not* choose to disclose his LD and does not request needed accommodations, and if he is substandard in performance of his duties, he is vulnerable to being fired and will not fall under the protection of these laws. This is true even if the problems behind his poor work performance are disability-related. The bottom line is that he is not protected unless he self-discloses and self-advocates for what he needs in order to do his job well.

To disclose or not to disclose?

Disability law prohibits employers from asking at a job interview if an applicant has a disability; therefore, it will be up to your teen to decide whether or not to self-identify—either at the interview stage or after being hired—in order to take advantage of the guaranteed protections described above. Since there are trade-offs in each decision, he will need to weigh the pros and cons based on every new work scenario.

Many adults with LD are wary of disclosing, since learning disabilities are not generally well understood in society and are too often equated with mental retardation; even those who have a basic understanding of LD often fail to grasp the breadth of their effects. Concerned about the potential for job discrimination, lowered expectations, and fewer opportunities for job advancement, many workers with LD feel more comfortable avoiding self-disclosure with potential employers—at least until after they are hired—and prefer to work around the label.

One Woman's Strategy

Joanne thinks carefully about whether to disclose whenever she applies for a new position. Her first preference is to communicate her strong motivation to compensate for her weaknesses by letting her interviewer know what she needs ("I can be more productive if I have a quiet place where I can do my work without distractions.") and to avoid actually using the term *learning disability*.

Unfortunately, without disclosure, Joanne (in the above example) is not guaranteed protection under the ADA and Section 504. If she is unable to access the quiet space she needs on an informal basis, she will have to embark on the more formal process of self-disclosing, providing documentation of her LD, and identifying the quiet place to work as her needed accommodation. It is important for her to consider the consequence of *not* disclosing: Could she manage the job without this accommodation? If she does not self-disclose and secure the quiet workspace she needs, will she be misunderstood and accused of laziness and inconsistent effort?

All of these considerations are irrelevant for your teen if he lacks self-advocacy skills. Too many people with LD avoid self-disclosure because they lack an understanding of their own LD profile and are unclear about how to describe their problems or about which accommodations they should be requesting. Your child will be empowered by achieving the self-awareness and self-acceptance discussed earlier in this book, by becoming knowledgeable about the laws, and by receiving explicit training in how to self-advocate. If he is to take full advantage of these legal safeguards, he must:

✓ Know he has LD.

✓ Have written documentation that validates his diagnosis.

✓ Be aware that he qualifies for civil rights protection.

✓ Be able to identify accommodations that will enable him to perform his duties.

✓ Be willing to take the risk to self-identify.

Many employees with LD feel disclosure enhances their potential for success on the job and perceive it to be the best route to survival in the work place. Your child will need to make this very personal decision each time he seeks new employment, based upon his own profile of strengths and weaknesses and how they match with the particular job for which he is applying.

What accommodations could he ask for?

It's important that your teen be aware of the types of reasonable accommodations to which he might be entitled and understand that he should only ask for those he truly requires. Depending upon his documented needs, he may self-advocate for:

- *Modification of his workspace*—e.g., a distraction-free environment (optimally, a private office but, at a minimum, provision of earplugs, sound screens, or noise reduction headphones).

- *Modification of instructions*—e.g., instructions in writing, taped instructions that can be listened to repeatedly, checklists, oral directions delivered slowly, the opportunity to repeat directions back before undertaking tasks to make sure they've been understood.

- *Modification of supervision*—e.g., more frequent reviews and performance appraisals.

- *Modification of work schedules*—e.g., flextime, built-in breaks.

- *Modified equipment*—e.g., low- and high-tech devices, ranging from paper day planners to computer calendar software to voice synthesizers and scanners.

- *Modified materials*—e.g., exams and training materials provided on audio- or videotape.

- *Modified tasks*—e.g., restructuring the job itself: shifting responsibility to other employees for minor job tasks that an employee is unable to perform because of a disability, and altering when or how a job task is performed.

Accommodations that Worked

Glenn Young describes the set of accommodations that allow him to perform well at his job:

> I have a whole list of accommodations that are agreed to and signed off on. I am recognized as a person with a disability, and I am provided with the accommodations. My favorite is that under no circumstance will the condition of my desk be taken into consideration in my performance appraisal. That is written down, signed off, agreed to, all the way up the line.... This is the agreed accommodation—also that I will never have to hand-write in public; will never have to provide anything in a handwritten way; that even though my job grade level is not such that I am entitled to secretarial support, for key documents that have to go out, I will have secretarial support to review, check for spelling, etc. Even though I am in a cubicle, if I need to, I can take over an office and use it in isolation. These things allow me to be functional in the workplace (Roffman 2000, 270).

Beyond accommodations, there are a variety of "people-supports" that may be used to enhance a new worker's adjustment to a job. Many students with LD and other disabilities begin their work lives in *supported employment,* in which they benefit from on-site assistance from an employment training specialist, job coach, or vocational instructor who helps them find an appropriate position, provides one-on-one guidance and advice about any needed accommodations, and helps them adjust to the social and vocational demands of their position. Such formal supports, which may be offered short-term or continue over an extended period of time, are generally funded by the local school system or by the Department of Vocational Rehabilitation. The ultimate goal is to phase out these external supports or use them only when the individual embarks upon a new position and to phase into use of available *natural supports.*

Natural supports are existing supports, such as computer training workshops available to all employees. Specific coworkers or supervisors already on the job can be natural supports as well, if an employee who discloses his LD to his employer grants permission to share with other employees what is otherwise considered to be confidential information about his disability. With your child's express permission, a coworker could be informed about his LD-related needs and provide assistance.

Natural Supports in Action

The use of natural supports promotes positive relationships with other workers and enables employees with LD to take on more typical work roles. For example, John tends to lose track of time and would be late for meetings if it were not for Tanisha, who works with him and gives him a warning that their meeting is about to begin in ten minutes. May is a fine writer but spells poorly. After she runs a spell check on her documents, a coworker always double-checks for uncorrected errors. These and other such natural supports are relatively easy to cultivate and often result in positive relationships with coworkers.

Parent tips regarding accommodations and supports

☞ As a parent, you should become familiar with disability-related laws and how they will affect your child as he enters the workplace.

☞ Advise your teen to check out the Job Accommodation Network (JAN), a federally funded resource that offers individualized consultation about accommodations. Your teen may use the JAN services whenever he begins a new job in which he thinks he may need to receive accommodations. He may visit JanWeb.wva.edu on the Web or call 800-ADA-WORK and speak with a Human Factors Consultant who will conduct a computer search for information based on the functional requirements of the specific job he has been hired to perform, his functional limitations, environmental factors, and other information. The consultant will provide information reflecting "close-to-matching" situations along with the names, addresses, and phone numbers of appropriate resources for more insights. JAN services are provided at no cost. All that is required of your teen is a list of the accommodations he actually uses, which is entered into the JAN's database and shared with others as needed.

☞ Be available to listen to and support your teen as he decides what he wants to do, where he wants to work, whether he plans to self-disclose, and how he plans to self-advocate. Above all else, your teen will benefit from feeling supported.

More about Vocational Rehabilitation (VR)

An important resource in the transition planning process is the Department of Vocational Rehabilitation, known in some states as the Office of Vocational Rehabilitation. This adult service agency helps individuals with disabilities meet their employment goals and find work that matches their strengths, interests, and abilities. Each state has a Vocational Rehabilitation agency that is funded by both the federal government (80 percent) and the state government (20 percent) to provide local VR services.

VR agency representatives are available to attend IEP meetings and consult with school staff members to identify students who may be eligible for their services. Talk with your school staff about asking a representative to attend your teen's meeting. At the least, your teen with LD should be aware of this resource, which may be of assistance not only while he is still in high school but also later in his adult life. (It is important that you remember, however, that while services for your child have been an entitlement during his K–12 schooling, they will be available solely based on eligibility and availability in the years that follow his exit from high school.)

An individual with disabilities can self-refer for VR assistance or be referred by anyone familiar with him, including his parents or school personnel. If your teen is referred for VR assistance, you can expect the following:

- A VR counselor assigned to his case will interview him to determine whether he is eligible to receive services. The criteria for eligibility include having a physical or mental impairment that results in a substantial impediment to employment; having the potential to benefit from the agency's services to attain employment (officially termed *the presumption of benefit*); and needing VR services to prepare for, enter, engage in, or retain gainful employment.

- The counselor will assess his work history, education and training, strengths, interests, VR needs, and employment goals, and will work with him to develop an Individualized Plan for Employment (IPE), which will be reviewed annually. The IPE outlines his goals and what he needs in terms of VR services and on-the-job assistance. It describes how services will be provided, how his progress will be evaluated, and the services to be provided after he obtains a job (including counseling and other supports, such as job coaching) for a period of three months.

Once it has been determined that your child is eligible for VR services, his VR counselor will consider your family resources and level of need. Commensurate with your means, your family may be expected to share in costs of services such as attending college and purchasing equipment. Financial need is not considered for counseling, guidance, plan development, or job placement. Your counselor will discuss financial planning as part of developing the IPE.

VR may conduct a comprehensive vocational assessment, provide community-based work experiences, or pay for vocational exploration and career development supports. Services include training to help students learn skills needed for identified job matches as well as payment for all books, tools, and equipment needed in the process. VR also provides assistive technology to enable students to perform job tasks. Perhaps the most frequently sought services are job placement and supports.

Parent tips for seeking VR services

☞ If you are planning on seeking services, VR strongly recommends that your teen be referred as part of his Individualized Education Program planning process to the public Vocational Rehabilitation Program in your area two years prior to his anticipated graduation from high school. This timing allows the vocational rehabilitation counselor time to work with you, the school, and your child to help identify a suitable work goal and suggest work readiness activities that should be taking place during high school. Before your teen leaves school, the VR counselor will develop an Individualized Plan for Employment (IPE) to arrange for additional training, education, or job placement services needed beyond school.

☞ Individuals receiving Social Security Income (SSI) may take advantage of the Plan for Achieving Self-Support (PASS) program, a work incentive program that allows people with disabilities to set aside income or resources for a specified period of time to achieve a work goal (e.g., for postsecondary learning, for a job coach, or for job-related equipment). Like a transition plan, a PASS is very individualized and establishes job-related goals and objectives. A PASS can be incorporated into your child's Individualized Education Program. To qualify, an individual must be currently receiving SSI benefits, have a feasible and reasonable occupational goal and a defined timetable, need income or resources other than SSI benefits to be set aside, and be prepared to explain anticipated expenditures of the reserved funds. PASS applications are available at your child's special education office or the local Social Security Administration office; work with your VR office to develop a plan and submit the application.

☞ If your child is eligible for SSI, he should learn more about SSI work incentives that encourage individuals on government assistance to become financially independent. Some students with LD may qualify for additional services from Social Security. For information, visit **SSA.gov**.

GAINING EMPLOYMENT IN SEVEN STEPS

As discussed at the opening of this chapter, the path to successful employment begins in early childhood and entails a number of important steps. After your child becomes more self-aware and self-accepting, he can begin to develop an understanding of why and how people work—and ultimately envision how he can become a thriving, contributing member of the workforce.

Step one: Developing self-awareness

Self-awareness informs the process of career planning and is one of the building blocks of healthy life adjustment. You, your teen, and his teachers can work together to help him become more self-aware by identifying what he enjoys doing, what he does well, and what he finds difficult.

Parent tips for raising self-awareness

☞ Have your child jot down his answers to the questions in Figure 1. You do the same (about him) on a separate sheet of paper. Discuss the similarities and differences in your responses. These will provide valuable input to the career assessment (discussed later in this chapter) conducted as part of his transition planning.

FIGURE 1

Raising Your Self-Awareness

Interests

- What are your favorite subjects in school?
- What hobbies and free-time activities do you enjoy?
- What are you interested in learning more about in the future?
- In which activities do you have a special talent and tend to do very well?

Memory

- Do you remember what people ask of you?
- When you are learning new tasks, which is stronger—your memory for what you see or your memory for what you hear?

Interpersonal skills

- How comfortable are you in social situations?
- What kinds of social situations are most difficult for you?
- Do you get along with others?
- Do you work well as a member of a team?
- When you are on a team, which role fits you best (leader, note-taker, presenter)?

Work aptitudes

- How do you do with planning, prioritizing, and organizing?
- Do you tend to improve on tasks with practice?
- Do you tend to work better when you can sit quietly for long periods of time, or do you prefer tasks that allow you to move around?

Motivation

- How motivated are you?
- What kinds of activities motivate you the most?
- Are you able to follow through, even on tasks that are not always motivating?

Basic skills

- Do you consider reading to be a strength or a weakness?
- Do you consider writing to be a strength or a weakness?
- Do you consider math to be a strength or a weakness?

Motor skills

- Are you good with your hands?
- Do you do well on fine-motor tasks that involve your fingers, such as typing?
- How do you do with gross-motor tasks that involve your arms and legs, such as using ladders or driving?

Answering these questions will serve both to raise self-awareness and to begin the career planning process. As your teen becomes more self-attuned, he will become aware of strengths and interests upon which he might build career plans. Knowing that his spatial perception is a strength and that he loves to tinker with machines and equipment, for example, could lead him toward positions that call upon those skills.

> As soon as you can, find out what you really like in life and focus on it as hard as you can. Try to read...everything you can about...the subjects that you really like. That's what I did with investments. I really liked it when I was 13, and I got to like it more as I went along in life...but I'm not good in other things. So that's okay. It's okay to specialize.
>
> Charles Schwab. "Kids Quiz Charles Schwab about the Personal Side of Learning Disabilities."
> SchwabLearning.org/teens

Recognizing how his disability could *negatively* affect his job performance will also help your child make more informed career choices. It will steer him away from positions mismatched to his particular profile of strengths and challenges. If he has problems writing in school, for example, he would be wise to avoid writing-intensive jobs or positions that place a premium on strong writing skills. If he is aware that his distractibility could get in the way at work, he should understand that working in a cubicle will not serve him well.

Step two: Developing self-acceptance

Once your child has established a foundation of self-awareness, self-acceptance is an attainable goal. Arriving at self-acceptance is a hard-won struggle for us all, but particularly for adolescents whose battles with self-image (related to their appearance and relationships) are legend. Teenagers generally shy away from being different in any way from their peers; this is especially true of those who have learning disabilities. It is not unusual for the middle school or early high school student with LD to deny the need for any special services and to balk at the label *learning disabled*.

Part of your child's journey into adult life, however, entails coming to terms with the fact that he does have a learning disability—that it's part of who he is and will need to be dealt with in day-to-day life and work; that its effects are not limited to school; and that it's not going away. He needs to come to see the *yin and yang* of LD, that along with his weaknesses, he has strengths, and that some of those strengths may in fact be directly attributable to the LD itself. Accepting this is an ongoing process very much tied to developing self-awareness. As Gerber and Reiff conducted research on factors that contributed to success in employment among adults with LD, they found that "once they accepted their LD and its challenges, they were 'freed up' to take on the many demands of the workplace" (1994, 99). Supporting and encouraging this *reframing* will help your teen prepare to meet challenges not only in employment, but in other aspects of adult life as well.

Step three: Developing an understanding of why people work

Before he can acknowledge the importance of preparing for a career and become motivated for the process ahead, your teen will need to develop an understanding of the benefits enjoyed by those who work. The financial benefits will be the most obvious to him, as he has likely saved up for items he has wanted to buy and can readily see that nachos and Nikes both come at a price. He should also come to understand the sense of fulfillment that employees gain from developing, executing, and successfully completing projects. Working is more than just a means of support; it also endows individuals with a sense of purpose.

Parent tips for promoting an understanding of why people work

Discuss the social benefits of employment with your child. Talk about the relationships built at work, the positive regard earned from others when a person has a job, and the boost to self-esteem that will come when he knows he has obtained and maintained employment and regularly brings home a paycheck.

Discuss elements of jobs you have held that you have found fulfilling and that have boosted your sense of accomplishment. You don't have to hide the fact that you have experienced bad days at work as well as good—but do share some of the satisfaction that employment has brought.

Step four: Developing career awareness

In order to develop a vision of his future employment, your teen first has to develop a sense of the kinds of jobs that are out there. This isn't easy. Because there are very few mechanisms by which students may efficiently access information about all possible jobs and what they entail, it is often difficult for them to make informed choices about employment to explore.

Check out PrincetonReview.com for information about hundreds of careers—including descriptions, salary information, and necessary preparatory course work. There's also a career quiz on the site to help teens identify their work interests and styles.

Urge your child's school to infuse career awareness into the curriculum and to sponsor career fairs where students can learn about a range of employment options and meet potential employers. If your teen needs assistance in this area, ask to have goals related to career awareness built directly into his IEP. Beyond the resources of special education, be sure to take advantage of the services and materials in place for *all* students, not just students with LD. Public school guidance personnel (rather than special education personnel) often have access to fairly sophisticated computer programs and vocational assessment instruments that may raise your teen's career awareness.

So if you have an LD, what kind of job can you expect to get when you graduate?

Here's what my dad's always telling me: "Life isn't school, Boone." What he means is, having a learning difficulty might mean you don't do well in certain classes, but it doesn't mean you can't do well in life when you're out of school. Think about all the stuff you're good at. Maybe you've got a great memory or you're creative or you can fix things or whatever. Now think about all the great jobs that use those skills (visual montage: lawyer, teacher, carpenter, artist, fireman, etc.). You just need to figure out the best match for you.

Boone, Virtual Teen Mentor, on **SparkTop.org**

Parent tips for promoting career awareness

👉 Talk about various jobs with your child. Be sure he knows the titles and basic job responsibilities of all of his family members. As he gets older, increase the sophistication of your discussions about the work world so they include educational and skill requirements for various positions.

👉 Encourage your teen to talk with people who have jobs that interest him. It can be very helpful to conduct informational interviews of your neighbors, your friends, the parents of his friends, graduates of his high school, or local business contacts.

👉 Listen to your child's career goals with respect. It's important to have high expectations, but also to help your teen be realistic. If his dream job is attainable, help him develop a career track toward the position he desires. If his LD or the job market itself might make entry into his dream job too difficult, try to identify which elements appeal to him, and help him determine how he might enjoy their essence in other positions. For example, if he loves animals and wants to be a veterinarian but that isn't an attainable career goal, encourage him to look at the qualifications for that position and at the type of studies entailed in the training. If these seem prohibitively challenging, he could be redirected toward other animal-related positions, such as veterinary assistant, pet groomer, animal control officer, or dog walker.

As he becomes familiar with a range of job options, he will also learn about variability in work schedules, work environments, and other factors that have the potential to influence his career choice.

Answering the questions in Figure 2 may help him home in on a well-chosen career path.

FIGURE 2

Learning More About Myself as a Worker

What's important to me in a job? (*Check all that apply.*)

___Type of work

___Location

    ___Near home ___ In the city ___In the country

___Availability of transportation to and from work

___Work environment

    ___A quiet environment ___A bustling environment

___Hours worked

___Traditional hours (Monday–Friday, 9:00 A.M.–5:00 P.M.)

___Nontraditional hours (weekends, nights)

___Wages

___Amount of supervision

Other:_____

What motivates me to work? (*Check all that apply.*)

___Making money

___Being with people

___Being with animals

___Working for a special cause I care about

(which is_____)

___Gaining status

___Getting experience in a particular field

(which is_____)

Other:_____

What kinds of supports do I need for a job?
(*Check all that apply.*)

___Daily check-ins with a supervisor, at least at first

___Checklists of duties

___Assistive technology

___Job coaching

___Help with time management

___Help with reading

___Help with writing

___Help with organization

Other:_____

> **What types of tasks am I interested in doing?**
> (*Check all that apply.*)
>
> ___Lots of different tasks
>
> ___The same few tasks repeated often
>
> ___Tasks that involve teamwork
>
> ___Work that involves dealing with clients/customers
>
> ___Work that involves dealing with animals
>
> ___Physical tasks
>
> ___Outdoors work
>
> ___Work that involves travel
>
> Other:_____

Career awareness builds on self-awareness. Once your teen has a sense of himself and an understanding of the qualifications required for a range of possible jobs, he will be better informed and in a stronger position to align his skills and interests with well-matched potential employment.

Step five: Career exploration

Your child will benefit immensely from engaging in active career exploration while he is still in high school. Many districts offer opportunities for school-based jobs, such as helping in the main office, assisting with custodial or landscaping services, providing peer support in the media center, or participating in a school-based enterprise, such as a photocopy center or school store. Although school-based jobs provide the chance to try out work skills within a supportive environment, the lack of real-world expectations and job tasks limits their effectiveness as an avenue for career exploration. While they may represent a good starting place on the road to employment, they are not authentic enough to meet a student's career training needs entirely.

Opportunities to work at community-based jobs are less commonly offered by schools, mostly because the logistics involved in providing students with transportation and site-based supervision can be complicated and expensive. However, real-world training within the community is more powerful than training in simulated settings. When students practice work skills within their community, they benefit from increased social integration and have a greater opportunity to practice using social skills with coworkers who do not have disabilities. They also develop a better understanding of the rationale behind the work in which they are engaged and are more likely to generalize the skills they learn and use them in the future.

Community-based job training comes in many shapes and sizes. Many school systems offer half-day job *internships* that allow students to work for several weeks or months at jobs of interest to them. These students typically attend academic classes in the morning and then go to work several days a week at a local day care center, auto body shop, landscaping service, or other community setting, where they assume the responsibilities of an employee and benefit from on-the-job training and supervision. Some schools help students find *apprenticeships*, extended training opportunities under the supervision of experienced workers in highly skilled trades, such as cabinetry. Your child's school may also offer less time-intensive career exploration opportunities such as *job shadowing*, which entails working alongside an employee to develop a sense of what that person's position involves. A student may participate in job shadowing for as little as a day or for an extended period of time. A series of job shadowing experiences would offer your teen a window into a variety of occupations.

A Word about Job Training

Job training should include the opportunity to develop skills for your teen's particular job placement. His school should provide workplace literacy training, teaching him how to fill out work-related forms, how to do specific writing tasks required for his position, how to spell essential words used on his job, and how to read materials needed for his work.

Your teen is entitled to thoughtful work placement based upon careful assessment in the career exploration process. He should be offered a choice among training opportunities, since self-determination in job selection fosters greater long-term vocational success; individuals with disabilities tend to be less motivated when placed in non-preferred jobs and are less likely to maintain them. When your teen begins his placement, he should receive a full orientation to the environment, people, and tasks of the job. Clear records should be maintained of the hours he works and of his progress toward his goals. The school and worksite should carefully plan the duties your teen performs, and they should relate to the transition goals set on his IEP. His performance should be assessed both in relation to his IEP goals and in comparison to the work of the average employee at his job site. If there is no school staff member present during his work hours, an on-site supervisor should be designated and present whenever he is there. The on-site supervisor, who will understand better than anyone what it means to be successful at this particular job, should work collaboratively with school personnel to develop an assessment device to evaluate your teen's performance on the job. Throughout the process, encourage him to self-advocate for accommodations or for more frequent assessments, if necessary. Praise his progress, and be available to support him.

Vocational School Opportunities

During the transition planning process, families should consider whether local vocational school offerings might meet their child's needs. Some states offer an excellent variety of programs designed for students both with and without special needs. In New Jersey, for instance, the County Vocational School System provides a number of hands-on learning experiences that take the form of "shared time" programs coordinated with the local public school district. Following a thorough vocational evaluation, typically administered during the eighth-grade year, students may qualify for employment orientation, skills training, job shadowing/internships, cooperative industrial education, and additional vocational exploration. A broad selection of programs is available throughout a special education student's four-year high school career in areas such as auto servicing, food preparation, building maintenance/home repair, cabinetmaking, hospitality, landscaping, and graphic services. Participation in these vocational experiences does not preclude the possibility of postsecondary academic education experiences at two-year or four-year college programs; with good planning and input from district guidance counselors, pursuing a college degree is also an achievable goal.

Parent tips for promoting career exploration

By high school, you should be encouraging your child to explore his skills and interests through after-school and/or summer jobs. If paid work is not available, volunteer work and community service will help him develop a sense of how the work world functions and how he might fit into it. Volunteer work will also enable him to begin to develop a work history. He can pursue his interests and meet new people, all while making a contribution to the community. If he wants and needs your support, help him fill out applications, plan appropriate interview attire, and discuss social skills for his particular work setting.

Once your teen has a job, encourage him to self-advocate for a clear explanation of his own responsibilities and expectations as well as those of his supervisor; a list of other workers with whom he will interact and their roles; and a written list of the rules of the workplace, such as how employees handle absences, tardiness, or personal emergencies.

Encourage him to talk about his workdays. Try to just listen and avoid jumping in too often with unsolicited advice. His supervisor will make suggestions—your job is to help him process his days and to cheer on his efforts.

Step six: Career preparation

A thorough career assessment is an essential ingredient to appropriate transition planning in the employment domain. A full career assessment involves gathering information based on formal vocational tests, surveys, and inventories; interviews with you, your teen, and his teachers (about your answers to the questions in Figures 1 and 2 and other observations and insights); and feedback from any job supervisors he has had. A good assessment should yield information about your teen with regard to:

→ **Career-related aptitudes:** Is he mechanical? Artistic?

→ **Temperament:** Is he people-oriented? Patient? Easygoing? Irritable when stressed?

→ **Learning styles:** Does he learn new skills best by hearing about them? By seeing them demonstrated? By being walked through new tasks, step-by-step?

→ **Work skills:** Is he able to sustain attention to a task and follow it through to completion? Does he understand the importance of reliability, dependability, flexibility, honesty, and a positive attitude? Is he able to demonstrate these qualities on a job?

→ **Basic skills:** How are his reading, writing, and math skills? As a component of vocational preparation, he may need help with *work literacy*—reading manuals and other materials, writing documents and invoices, or using math to measure or manage money.

Functional life skills: Does he have the following skills needed for work?

- **Mobility/ability to move efficiently from place to place:** Can he get where he needs to go on his own by car, bicycle, or public transportation? Is he capable of traveling to and from a job or training site? Is he likely to get lost because he cannot remember landmarks? Will he have difficulty reading signs or maps? How is his sense of direction?

- **Communication:** Does he have trouble processing directions? Will he have difficulty interpreting memos or manuals, completing job applications, writing reports or letters, or relaying information to coworkers?

- **Interpersonal skills:** There are myriad social skills required in work environments, including being able to participate in both formal and informal conversation, getting along with and being supportive of others, accepting criticism, taking direction, making/refusing requests, and recognizing the physical and emotional personal boundaries of coworkers. Is he capable of interacting in a socially acceptable and mature manner with coworkers, supervisors, and others? Is he able to interpret the facial expressions, tones of voice, and other nonverbal cues of others? Does he understand the impact of his own nonverbal communication? How capable is he of working collaboratively?

- **Self-care:** Is he independently able to manage any medications he needs to take? How are his grooming and hygiene? Does he understand that his personal appearance will contribute significantly to the impression he makes on others at work and that he may need to make compromises regarding piercings, clothing choices, and hairstyles based upon the type of position he is seeking?

- **Executive functioning (planning, organizing, prioritizing):** How well does he do with planning, organizing, and prioritizing? How is his time management? Does he have problems with follow-through?

- **Work tolerance:** Is he able to sustain an adequate work pace over an extended period of time, particularly under pressure?

Once your teen has developed his self-awareness, explored his areas of interest, and received the results of his career assessment, he should be fully prepared to consider his interests and self-perceptions together with his established aptitudes to determine jobs for which he is well suited and at which he would excel.

Parent tips for promoting career preparation

☞ Work with your teen to select courses that will help him prepare for a job in the fields that appeal to him. If, for example, he is interested in carpentry, he will need to develop strong math skills. If he would like to pursue a career in medicine, he will need a well-planned college-preparation curriculum with a solid base of science courses.

☞ Help him understand that the process of setting and working actively toward specific goals will help him move forward in employment.

With or without an LD, just wanting to be something isn't enough. You've got to set a goal, stay focused, and work really, really hard to get there. Maybe that's where having an LD can help. None of us would be where we are right now if we didn't set goals, stay focused and work really, really hard every single day of our lives.

Mia, Virtual Teen Mentor, on SparkTop.org

Step seven: Finding a job and assimilating into the work world

Not surprisingly, the best way to develop job skills is on a job. Although taking an unpaid position is a good and necessary first step to employment for many students, working for pay during high school has proven to have a positive long-term career impact on individuals with LD.

When your teen looks for employment, it's very important that he try to find a job that:

- Interests him.
- Allows him to work around his weaknesses—with accommodations, if needed.
- Lets him take advantage of his strengths.
- Has a supportive supervisor and coworkers.
- Is within a work climate accepting of diversity.

Gerber (1992, 482) refers to this matching as *goodness of fit* and emphasizes its importance in successful adjustment to employment.

Your teen's school should teach him job-search skills, an activity that may be included in his IEP objectives. He needs to know how to decipher newspaper want ads and online listings; network (since most special education students who work after high school find jobs via connections); complete application forms; write and update his resume; write a cover letter to send along with his resume; write a thank-you letter after interviews; and conduct a job interview by answering questions, asking questions, and attending to both his own and his interviewer's body language.

> There's not much worse than an applicant's wearing a baseball cap or a team jacket to a job interview. When you go to an interview, you want to be neutral and professional.
> Dr. Robert K. Mulligan, Director, Special Education, Point Pleasant Beach School District, New Jersey

> The interview process is difficult for many [people with LD, who] must make sure that their difficulties with directions, transportation, utilizing time, and organizing themselves do not cause them to be late. Their grooming must be excellent, a challenging process for some people who have visual perception problems and fine-motor coordination difficulties. And, of course, the job interview itself is a set of complex social skills, which can be problematic for those with language disabilities or problems relating to others.
> Dale Brown and Paul Jay Gerber. "Employing People with Learning Disabilities." (1995, 196).

Some high schools sponsor job clubs as an organized support for students in search of employment. Composed entirely of individuals who are looking for work, job club members meet regularly to update their resumes, practice interviewing, and provide mutual support. Meetings are usually structured with an activity or discussion around a related topic (such as interviewing), and a time set at the end for each member to report on progress toward his individual goals. Often sponsored by the local VR office, job clubs provide an excellent opportunity to practice goal setting and other self-determination skills, establish peer support networks, and practice using the interpersonal skills needed for work and community life.

Parent tips for developing job-search skills

Call upon any connections you have, and help your teen network for a job among your family and friends.

Suggest that he pick up two copies of job applications for any positions he wishes to pursue so he can use one as a draft. Urge him to carry a completed generic application as a sample when he goes to visit potential employers, but let him know that it is reasonable to ask to be able to take an application home to complete and return later. Alert him that handwriting and spelling do "count" when it comes to applying for a job.

Discuss the elements of job interviews with your teen. If he's willing to role-play, practice handshakes that are neither too firm nor too limp, and insist on good eye contact. Ask questions that require him to self-advocate, including, "Tell me about your strengths and weaknesses for this job." Help him prepare a few appropriate questions to ask you in your role as mock interviewer. You may find it helpful to start by taking the role of applicant and letting him do the interviewing; this gives you the chance to model effective interview behavior.

If your child will allow it and you have the equipment, videotape a practice interview; watch it and have him critique his own body language, his responses to your questions, and the questions he asked. Then have him complete the interview again, this time incorporating his own suggested changes.

As your teen seeks employment after high school or college, he may choose to take advantage of the services of One-Stop Career Centers, located all across the United States. These offer a variety of free career development and job search services. Funded by the U.S. Department of Labor, centers are required to meet the needs of all job seekers who want to use them. They provide job postings, computer stations with access to the Internet, information about different types of jobs, support groups for job seekers, job fairs, and workshops on such job-seeking skills as resume writing and interviewing. Information regarding local services is available at ServiceLocator.org or 877-872-5627.

With self-awareness, your teen will be better prepared to develop strategies that will help him work around his weaknesses. If he has time management problems, for example, he might plan to build in a "catch-up" period—an extra cushion of time to meet deadlines—at the end of each day. If he tends to procrastinate, he may choose to set benchmarks and reward himself for goals he meets (e.g., "I'll take a break when I finish this memo"). If he has memory problems, he may decide to jot down multiple-step directions, a solution that will help avoid incurring the wrath of supervisors who only see lack of follow-through and don't understand the impact of weak auditory memory.

> *The way I manage my job is through lists and colored folders. I over-organize, or I'd be lost.*
> A teacher with a learning disability, personal communication

Parent tips for promoting career assimilation

☞ Encourage your teen to maintain a vocational history file in the Transition Planning Portfolio described earlier in Chapter 5. The file should include a listing of all of his work experiences, including paid and unpaid positions, the names of the companies or organizations where he has worked, the dates he worked, his title, his responsibilities, and the names of his supervisors. As he moves on from each job, he should ask his supervisor for a written letter of recommendation, which should also be kept in his Transition Planning Portfolio. He will be able to use these as evidence of his work experience with future employers.

☞ Help your teen think about his career trajectory. What experiences will he need to have under his belt in order to move on to the next step in his career? Once he's demonstrated competence in a position, encourage him to seek out additional responsibilities at work that will provide him with valuable experience.

Q & A

Q. Should people include bad work experiences on their resume?

A. *It all depends. If it was a brief summer job I'd leave it off. If the person was fired and he'd worked with that employer for a significant amount of time, he'd have to explain the gap in employment history anyway, so he might as well leave it on. If the experience was bad because the job match wasn't good and the person decided to leave on his own, then maybe he should include that job on the resume and explain the circumstances with a positive spin in his interview.*

Interview with Jim Sarno, Area Director, Massachusetts Rehabilitation Commission

Career development: A case study

Darlene's story provides an example of the possible ups and downs in the career development of a young person with LD.

Case Study

Darlene had always loved children. Following a career assessment conducted by her transition counselor at school, she was offered the choice of working two days per week at either a local day care center or at the town library's children's room. Darlene chose the former, which was a short bus ride from her home. Her high school's career ed class helped prepare her for the placement by teaching her how to use public

---

transportation, by having her practice her self-advocacy skills, and by giving her opportunities to role-play job interviews. Darlene decided to disclose her LD at the interview because she felt she would need accommodations in order to do her job well. In particular, she was concerned about her weak reading skills and asked that she be allowed to bring home books to practice reading them to herself before having to read to the children during circle time. She also asked for a proofreader to check the written documentation she was required to provide when behavioral problems arose among the children in her charge.

Darlene's biggest problem was adjusting to the transition from *service receiver* to *service provider*. After years of special education in school—during which the world seemed to revolve around her needs—she found it hard to move beyond her self-centeredness and consistently place the needs of the children before her own. Sometimes she regressed to the level of the toddlers, arguing like a three-year-old with no sense of the loss of her professional stature. At other times, she was withdrawn and passive, waiting to be comforted, forgetting that she was no longer the client and that she was now in the giving rather than the receiving role. With much supervision at daily feedback sessions and many gentle reminders from both an on-site supervisor and a vocational counselor from her high school, Darlene grew beyond her egocentrism and became more attuned to the needs of the children.

She still needed to work on the social skills necessary for success in the workplace, however. Darlene was uncomfortable with adults. She rarely greeted the other teachers, and when she did, her eyes were often downcast and her voice barely audible. She often sat alone in the lunchroom. On the occasions when she found it necessary to speak with the other teachers, she was often inattentive to the social cues indicating that they were busy, and she would interrupt their conversations. Through an intensive social skills training class built into her transition plan along with supervision targeted to learning to relate to other adults, Darlene gradually developed the ability to assert herself more appropriately at work. She grew to recognize and understand body language, and she developed skills to carry on social conversation with colleagues.

Darlene's progress was exceptional. Her practice reading at home prepared her well for circle time, and she benefited from the caring natural support of a coworker who proofread any written work required of her.

Other problems arose throughout her training, though. She was not always able to use sound reasoning and once became offended that she was expected to wash tables after snack, indignantly declaring, "I'm here to work with children!" Another time, she failed to contact her supervisor when she was sick, using the excuse that the line had been busy when she phoned at 8:00 A.M., and that at least she had "tried." Each incident presented a learning opportunity for Darlene, and through supervision and advising, she was able to better understand the nature of her responsibility as a day care aide.

After two years of work and supervision, Darlene developed into a fine aide and, upon graduation from high school, was offered a paid position as an assistant teacher. She is immensely proud of her achievement, and indeed she should be—all of her hard work paid off, and she landed the job she'd sought.

SUMMARY

Self-determination sits at the center of vocational transition planning. In order to be able to take control over their choices and decisions about their work lives, adolescents with LD must have a clear sense of their strengths, weaknesses, interests, and the type of environment in which they might work best. They must also be aware of the laws that protect them from discrimination at work, know what accommodations might help them perform best on the job, and understand the pros and cons of self-disclosure.

In order to develop career readiness, your teen needs to progress through the seven steps outlined in this chapter, including becoming self-aware, recognizing and accepting his LD, developing an understanding of the benefits of being employed, learning about jobs that match his interests and aptitudes, exploring possible job matches, and developing the prevocational and vocational skills that will enable him to search for and maintain employment. Careful transition planning can help your child progress through these steps, learn much both about himself and about the work world, and develop the motivation and skills to enter the job market and be successful.

CHAPTER 7

AIMING FOR SUCCESS AND QUALITY OF LIFE

Success is a slippery concept; it's hard to define, largely because, as Dr. Marshall Raskind, Director of Research and Special Projects at Schwab Learning, writes, "it means different things to different people and it may mean different things at different times in a person's life" ("Expert Answers Guide: Success Attributes of Kids with Learning Disabilities"). Yet somehow, we all strive for that golden ring and certainly want our children to achieve success, however that may be defined in our minds (and theirs). Generally we consider a person successful if she has friends and positive family relationships, is working in a satisfying position that pays the bills, and is healthy in body, mind, and spirit. Essentially, we might say that success is achieving quality of life.

This book has described what it means to have a learning disability in adolescence and has provided an overview of the transition process. It has discussed the move from high school into the community, into continued learning, and into the world of work. But how do we ensure that our children achieve a positive and rich quality of life? What can parents do to help their children prepare for a rich and satisfying—and successful—life? This chapter will address that topic.

DEFINING SUCCESS

In an effort to ferret out why some adults with LD fare well—socially, emotionally, educationally, occupationally—and others do not, several researchers have sought to identify the factors of success among individuals with learning disabilities.

At the Frostig Center in California, Dr. Raskind and his colleagues queried: *Why do some individuals with disabilities, end up doing well employment-wise, have good peer relations, family seems to be doing well, and who could be called "successful," while another group with similar backgrounds and similar types of disabilities may end up in really a difficult situation, barely able to keep their heads above water either emotionally, socially, or financially?*

Dr. Marshall Raskind. "How Do Kids with LD Become Successful?" SchwabLearning.org/teens

In a twenty-year longitudinal study of their graduates, the Frostig research team (Raskind, Goldberg, Higgins, and Herman, 1999) was able to pinpoint specific success attributes that contribute to what they had identified as successful life outcomes. In their reports on the results of their research, they note that, although successful individuals may not demonstrate all of the attributes, they tend to have more than those who are less successful.

The factors they identified and discussed below— self-awareness, proactivity, perseverance, goal setting, the presence and use of effective support systems, and emotional coping strategies—are very much in line with those earlier identified by Gerber, Ginsberg, and Reiff (1992), who looked at factors behind employment success in adults with LD. Your teen may well demonstrate some of these attributes already. Nonetheless, suggestions are included for how you can foster further development of these qualities and enhance your child's potential for success in adulthood.

Success and the Importance of Self-Awareness

As discussed throughout this book, it is critical that adolescents with learning disabilities develop self-awareness. By the time your teen leaves high school, she needs to be able to do the following:

- Recognize her strengths in both academic and non-academic realms, and take satisfaction in her talents.
- Know her limitations, again both in academic and non-academic areas.
- Identify her interests.

Once a person becomes aware that she has strengths as well as weaknesses, she can begin to recognize that there is more to her than her disability, and she can begin to accept and redefine herself in a more positive light. As Dr. Raskind writes, "It's one thing to be aware of your problems; it's another to be able to accept them, and that's another thing that we found with our successful individuals—they were able to do both" ("How Do Kids with LD Become Successful?").

Gerber et al. refer to this as reframing and describe this process as "reinterpreting the learning disabilities experience from something dysfunctional to something functional" (1996, 99). Reframing involves developing perspective about having a disability. As your teen starts to feel better about herself, her LD diagnosis will begin to take up less space in her self-concept.

Once a person is aware of her strengths and limitations and identifies her interests, she is well positioned to find her niche in life and to pursue work and leisure-time activities that complement her personal profile. Dr. Gerber's group found this "goodness of fit" to be a critical element in the success of adults with LD.

Self-awareness creates the foundation for a shift in attitude, a move toward self-acceptance, which builds into self-efficacy and increased self-esteem.

> *What you see in the mirror is important. If you see a person who cannot spell or cannot read well, you are looking at a handicapped person. If you see a person who is creative and has unique abilities, you are looking at a human being with potential.*
> Christopher M. Lee and Rosemary F. Jackson. *Faking It: A Look into the Mind of a Creative Learner* (122).

Self-awareness will also enable your child to begin working around her difficulties. Once she recognizes that she is disorganized, for example, she will understand that she needs to establish systems and organizational strategies to help her manage her life. Once she becomes aware that she has problems of inattention, she can learn how to reduce distractions when important tasks are at hand. And it is only once she has achieved self-awareness that she can develop the self-advocacy skills that will enable her to seek accommodations in work and learning settings.

THE PROS OF PROACTIVITY

Being proactive means taking the initiative by *acting* rather than *reacting* to events. It means being involved in community activities and anticipating what's needed to make life work rather than waiting passively to see what happens. The proactive individual takes responsibility for her actions and self-advocates for what she needs.

> *This is one of the things that the successful individuals with learning disabilities were able to do. They were really a part of a number of communities. And with this involvement came the idea that they could control their own destiny, that they could affect the outcome of their lives. They were active players in their own lives, as opposed to many unsuccessful individuals who really responded to events, were passive in their lives, and were more 'victims.'*
>
> Dr. Marshall Raskind. "Specific Success Attributes Among Individuals with Learning Disabilities."
> SchwabLearning.org/teens

Controlling one's destiny was a key theme in the Gerber interviews as well; many of the adults talked about taking charge of their lives and adapting in order to move ahead.

Try to help your teen develop confidence to step into life in a proactive manner. Encourage her to express her thoughts, feelings, and wishes with assertiveness. Help her find ways to participate in school and community activities. If she's athletic, then sports teams are an obvious avenue to involvement. If not, delve into her areas of interest, and work on finding ways for her to pursue them within school, youth groups, and the community at large.

Foster proactive decision-making in your child. Throughout these chapters, the importance of self-determination has been emphasized. It's critical that your teen have the opportunity to make choices, to take responsibility for her decisions, and to become confident enough to act upon them (e.g., "I'll do my chores before dinner so I can have a good stretch of time after I eat to write my report and still get to watch the TV show I love at 10:00 P.M."). It's also important for her to live with (and learn from!) the consequences of mistakes she makes.

Help your teen learn to think proactively. This is not an easy proposition, since most adolescents thrive on last-minute planning, but thinking ahead is an essential skill—and it's the basis of a proactive approach to life. Again, model through think-alouds (e.g., "I have to bring a dish to the pot-luck dinner in two days, but tomorrow's going to be really busy, so I'd better prepare it tonight."). Walk her through the thinking process for specific situations pending in her life (e.g., "If you go to the job fair at school on Thursday, prospective employers will probably want to see a resume. What do you need to do to polish yours up before then?"). A constructive line of questioning is far better than nagging, and it will help encourage her to practice the type of proactive thinking found to be so helpful among successful adults with LD.

THE VALUE OF PERSEVERANCE

Perseverance is old-fashioned "stick-to-it-iveness" or persistence. It means pursuing goals despite difficulties, viewing difficult situations as learning opportunities, and knowing how to deal with setbacks. Successful adults with LD often work harder than anyone else they know; for them, persistence is a way of life (Gerber et al. 1992, 482).

> *I'm struck by how the successful individuals also knew when they needed to shift gears. While they generally didn't give up on an overall goal, they knew when to back up a little bit or change the path a little bit to get there. The unsuccessful individuals, on the other hand, would just keep beating their heads against the wall and not recognize when it was time to reevaluate the strategies or, in some cases, the goal itself.*
>
> Dr. Marshall Raskind. "Specific Success Attributes Among Individuals with Learning Disabilities." SchwabLearning.org/teens

It's also important to note that sometimes perseverance entails recognizing when it's time to quit. Talk with your teen about the difference between perseverance and rigidity. This is not an easy distinction—your availability as a sounding board will be helpful when she is trying to decide whether it's time to accept that her goal needs to be changed and that her course of action should be altered.

It's important that your teen learn to recognize obstacles that keep her from achieving her goals and subsequently make a plan to overcome them (e.g., "I don't work well when I'm hungry, so if I really want to wrap up this report tonight, I should have a snack at around 9:00 P.M."). Help her learn to deal with and adjust to setbacks as she works toward her goals (e.g., "Okay, so my second draft of the application essay isn't quite good enough. I'll do one more draft, but this time I'll ask my English teacher first for a few hints on how to improve it."). It may be a relief for her to learn that sometimes succeeding is more a matter of savvy planning than of extreme perseverance—and that often it's a winning combination of the two.

GOAL SETTING

Goal setting or goal-orientation involves establishing objectives that are specific but that can be flexibly adapted if necessary. It entails understanding that objectives are achieved one step at a time, and it requires being able to prioritize the steps needed to reach a chosen aim.

Teens with LD must understand that goal-setting shapes the activities of our lives and helps us accomplish what we want and need to do. Working toward a goal can be very satisfying or very frustrating—in either case, a certain determination or drive is required to stay on course. Youth with LD often need support to learn to set and work toward goals effectively.

Encourage your teen to identify what she would like to accomplish, and then help her set specific goals. Keeping your own expectations high, help her determine whether her goals are realistic; if not, help her realign them to a more achievable level. Once she sets an attainable goal, be encouraging as she thinks through the various steps she must take and determines which should be tackled first (e.g., "There are a million jobs out there. If I want one, I need to look in the newspaper, check the online listings, write down the ones that might fit my skills and interests, contact the employers, and fill out applications. I guess I'd better start by getting a copy of today's newspaper.").

> *Goal setting feeds on itself. Once even minimal goals are achieved, the feelings of success that are bred can be the basis for more challenging goals in the future.*
> Paul Jay Gerber, Rick Ginsberg, and Henry B. Reiff. "Identifying Alterable Patterns in Employment Success for Highly Successful Adults with Learning Disabilities." (1992, 480).

THE PRESENCE AND USE OF EFFECTIVE SUPPORT SYSTEMS

According to Dr. Rashkind, it's crucial that your teen recognize when she needs help. She must develop the confidence and initiative to seek the support she needs and be willing to accept the assistance, guidance, and encouragement of others.

Support networks vary in composition. They may include family, friends, teachers, mentors, therapists, coworkers, clergy, and partners or spouses. Talk with your child about the people who stand behind her as a scaffold, and encourage her to take advantage of the assistance of her support system. Pointing out that she is part of your support network and that you have appreciated the various types of assistance she has offered you over the years will help her understand that support is reciprocal in healthy adult relationships.

Your teen needs to know that *all* people need help at times, and that there is no shame in seeking it; indeed, it is often a sign of maturity when a person steps forward and admits she needs assistance. Help her recognize available resources for everyday logistical support. Who can help her if she's confused at the bank? What can she do if she gets lost on the subway? To whom can she turn for help if she wants to get a driver's license? Use think-alouds ("How do I use this new kind of public transit ticket machine? Oh, there's a security guard I can ask.") to raise her awareness that you too scout out resources on a regular basis.

Being able to accept help yet avoid dependency is a fine balancing act; it requires that an individual also learn how to wean from supports once she no longer needs them. Many of the successful adults with LD in the Frostig study were able to achieve this balance (Raskind, "How Do Kids with LD Become Successful?").

COPING STRATEGIES

The Frostig research group found that, by and large, successful adults have developed effective means of coping with the emotional repercussions of their learning disability. It's important that your child be aware of how her emotions affect her behavior. How does she behave when she's angry? How does she manage pressure and the frustrations associated with her LD? As discussed in Chapter 2, Mental Health and Well-Being, it's crucial that she identify triggers of stress and recognize signs of overload. Does she feel it in her stomach? In her neck? Does she become irritable? Does she start engaging in unhealthy behaviors? Discuss this topic at length with your teen. Sharing some of your own triggers and coping strategies will help her see that she's not alone in her struggles with stress. Ultimately, she needs to develop a toolbox of coping strategies and be ready to use them against rising tension. She must also be able to discern when she needs outside support.

Successful adults also make use of practical strategies that help them cope with obstacles and reduce their stress in the process. Help your teen organize herself. As suggested in Chapter 4 on preparing for life in the community, assist her as she organizes her own space and encourage her to make a habit of mapping out her time. Help her plan ahead for both the routine and non-routine events in her life. Work with her to establish and maintain a calendar that lists all of her activities, and help her get into the habit of referring to it daily. Help her develop a time-planning hierarchy, delineating what gets first priority on the calendar (e.g., fill in school or work first, then medical appointments, then extracurricular activities, then other social plans and exercise). Once she fills in all of her scheduled activities, including the days her chores need to be done (e.g., Tuesday's garbage day), she will be able to see blocks of time available for studying and for leisure plans. Until she's ready to wean from regular support in this area, remind her to check her calendar to see what's ahead, and walk her through planning accordingly (e.g., "You're going to be at the barbeque until tonight. The forecast says it might rain—what can you do to prepare?"). Checklists, charts, and reminders posted on sticky-notes are all helpful tools she should regularly use.

Encourage her to make use of technology as a coping tool, as well. In recent years a number of wonderful technological innovations have become widely available, including text-to-speech software and PDAs. In my work with adults with LD, I hear again and again how computers have eased their lives. In my interviews for *Meeting the Challenge of Learning Disabilities in Adulthood*, one woman told me, "Spell-check is good…but delete is my friend because now I can write what I think, I can do what I want, and I'm not bogged down in any way by the burden of having to be right or almost right"

(2000, 292). Many websites offer helpful accommodations. For instance, Webster.com allows users to click on the speaker icon next to definitions and hear a word pronounced; CoolTimer at HarmonyHollow.net allows users to download a timer to their desktops. Watches and cell phones can serve as alarm clocks; tape recorders can be plugged into phones to take important messages. Technology does much to enhance quality of life for all—and particularly for adults with LD.

Achieving Good Quality of Life

In addition to the influence of the above attributes, your teen's quality of life will ultimately be affected by the characteristics of her LD and by her personal relationships. Because no two people have the same set of LD symptoms, the effect on quality of life is unique for each individual. Your teen will need to recognize the potential impact of her own set of symptoms and use her creative problem-solving skills to work around her limitations and build upon her strengths in order to enjoy good quality of life.

> As I watch my teenage son approach adulthood, I feel both protective and proud. Having struggled all his life with significant disabilities, he's learned lessons that I think would serve any young person well in the real world. Sometimes it seems that his reward for living a life with challenges is that he's gained greater insight and understanding than most teenagers have. He has worked hard and learned creative ways to manage his difficulties. He recognizes his strengths and plays to them. What am I most proud of when I look at my son? I think it is his sense of humility, humor, and compassion toward others. He respects authority, his peers—and himself. What more could any parent hope for?
>
> Katy, parent of Jim, age seventeen, personal communication

Additionally, connectedness to others has a direct effect on quality of life. Healthy relationships contribute to a fuller life experience. Family is important, and—increasingly, as your teen individuates—so are friendships. As she becomes engaged in the community and works to develop her social skills, she will be in a better position to cultivate relationships that will provide both company and personal validation.

Your teen may wonder if she'll ever have a long-term romantic relationship—especially how she might meet a potential partner, what topics they might talk about, how and when she will self-disclose, whether the partner will be able to see beyond the disability to who she truly is. She needs to hear that people with LD are perfectly capable of finding romance and developing long-term relationships. Many find partners, marry, and have children of their own. Her job now is to get as involved in community life as possible, to cultivate interests, to be a good listener with others, and to find two or three topics that she feels comfortable pursuing in conversation with others. Once she gets to know another person— whether friend or potential love interest—she will need to consider whether or not to disclose her disability. Having an open and frank discussion about how her LD affects her life will allow her to relax and worry less about managing her symptoms; and it will also lay the foundation for an honest relationship.

Your teen's quality of life will further be affected by her employment and financial status; this makes it all the more important that she eventually find a satisfying job and establish financial independence. As she progresses through the transition planning process, preparation for employment is of utmost importance and should be among the highest priorities. Your support will be crucial as your teen develops job readiness and assumes her place in the work world.

Your child's health will also have a significant impact on her future. For all of us—with or without learning disabilities— health contributes to quality of life. Although adolescents are known for eating a lot of pizza and for staying up until 4:00 A.M., it's important that you talk with your teen about eating well, exercising often, and otherwise practicing a healthy lifestyle. Your message may not have an immediate impact, but will very likely have a long-term influence.

Ultimately, quality of life depends upon an individual's relationship with herself. As your teen comes to terms with her LD and achieves self-understanding, self-acceptance, and self-determination, she will be in a stronger position to make a successful transition into the adult world.

APPENDIX

OPTIONS FOR ASSISTED INDEPENDENT LIVING

In The Princeton Review's *K&W Guide to Colleges for Students with Learning Disabilities or Attention Deficit Disorder*, 8th Edition (2007), authors Marybeth Kravets, MA, and Imy F. Wax, MS, provide the following table of assisted independent living options for young adults with LD and/or ADHD.

INDEPENDENT LIVING OPTIONS

The following programs are options for students who may have LD or ADHD or other disabilities, who want to continue to pursue independent living skills and education beyond high school.

ALLEN INSTITUTE CENTER FOR INNOVATIVE LIVING
85 Jones Street
PO Box 100
Hebron, CT 06248-0100
www.alleninstitute.info
mchaloux@alleninstitute.info
Phone: 866-666-6919
Fax: 866-228-9670

ANCHOR TO WINDWARD
66 Clifton Avenue
Marblehead, MA 01945
www.anchor-to-windward.org
info@anchortowindward.org
Phone: 781-693-0063
Fax: 781-639-9184

BANCROFT
Hopkins Lane
PO Box 20
Haddonfield, NJ 08033-0018
www.bancroft.org/html/contact.html
Phone: 856-429-0010 ext. 297

BERKSHIRE CENTER
18 Park Street
Lee, MA 01238
www.berskshirecenter.org
Phone: 413-243-2576
Fax: 413-243-3351

BREHM PREPARATORY SCHOOL
OPTIONS PROGRAM AT BREHM
1245 East Grand
Carbondale, IL 62901
www.brehm.org
Phone: 618-457-0371
Fax: 618-529-1248

CENTER FOR ADAPTIVE LEARNING
3350-A Clayton Road
Concord, CA 94519
www.centerforlearning.org
Phone: 925-827-3863

CHAPEL HAVEN
1040 Whalley Avenue
Westville, CT 06515
www.chapelhaven.org
Phone: 203-397-1714

CLOISTER CREEK
1280 Highway, 138 Southwest
Conyers, GA 30094
http://yp.bellsouth.com/sites/cloistercreek
Phone: 770-483-0748
Fax: 770-918-8217

EVALUATION AND DEVELOPMENTAL CENTER
Southern Illinois University
500-C South Lewis Lane
Carbondale, IL 62901
www.siu.edu/~rehabedc/support/edc_index.html
Phone: 618-453-2331

FOUNDATION FOR INDEPENDENT LIVING
5311 Northeast Thirty-third Avenue
Fort Lauderdale, FL 33308
www.filinc.org
csutherland@filinc.org
Phone: 954-968-6472

THE HORIZONS SCHOOL
2111 University Boulevard
Birmingham, AL 35233
www.horizonsschool.org
Phone: 205-322-6606 or 800-822-6242
Fax: 205-322-6605

INDEPENDENCE CENTER
3640 South Sepulveda Boulevard, Suite 102
Los Angeles, CA 90034
www.independencecenter.com
Phone: 310-202-7102
Fax: 310-202-7180

LIFE AT CAPE COD
550 Lincoln Road
Hyannis, MA 02601
www.lifecapecod.org/application.html
Phone: 508-790-3600

LIFE DEVELOPMENT INSTITUTE
18001 North Seventy-ninth Avenue, Suite E71
Glendale, AZ 85308
www.life-development-inst.org
ldomaroz@aol.com
Phone: 623-773-2774
Fax: 623-773-2788

LIFE SKILLS INC.
100 Highlands Way
Oxford, GA 30054
www.independentlivingga.com
Phone: 770-385-8913

LIVING INDEPENDENTLY FOREVER, INC.

LIFE GROUP LIVING
175 Great Neck Road South
Mashpee, MA 02649
www.lifecapecod.org/groupliving.html
Phone: 508-539-6979 or 508-477-6670

MAPLEBROOK SCHOOL
5142 Route 22
Amenia, NY 12501
www.maplebrookschool.org
mmbsecho@aol.com
Phone: 845-373-9511
Fax: 845-373-7029

Minnesota Life College
7501 Logan Avenue South, Suite 2A
Richfield, MN 55423
www.minnesotalifecollege.com
Phone: 612-869-4008
Fax: 612-869-0443

Moving Forward Toward Independence
1350 Elm Street
Napa, CA 94559
www.moving-forward.org
Phone: 707-251-8603

New York Institute of Technology
Independent Living Program
Central Islip Campus
Central Islip, NY 11722
info@vip-at-nyit.org
Phone: 631-348-3354
Fax: 631-348-0437

Pace Program
National-Louis University
2840 Sheridan Road
Evanston, IL 60201
www2.nl.edu/PACE
Phone: 847-256-5150

G.R.O.W. Project at Riverview School
549 Route 6A
East Sandwich, MA 02537
grow@riverviewschool.org
Phone: 508-888-3699
Fax: 508-833-7628

RIVERVIEW SCHOOL
551 Route 6A, Suite 1
East Sandwich, MA 02537
www.riverviewschool.org
admissions@riverviewschool.org
Phone: 508-888-0489
Fax: 508-833-7001

THRESHOLD PROGRAM AT LESLEY UNIVERSITY
29 Everett Street
Cambridge, MA 02138
www.lesly.edu
threshld@lesley.edu
Phone: 617-349-8181 or 800-999-1959 ext. 8181

VISTA VOCATIONAL & LIFE SKILLS CENTER
1356 Old Clinton Road
Westbrook, CT 06498
www.vistavocational.org/contact.html
Phone: 860-399-8080
Fax: 860-399-3103

CHILDREN AND ADULTS WITH ATTENTION-DEFICIT/ HYPERACTIVITY DISORDER (CHADD)
National nonprofit organization providing education, advocacy and support for individuals with ADHD.
www.chadd.org

COUNCIL FOR EXCEPTIONAL CHILDREN
International professional organization dedicated to improving educational outcomes for individuals with exceptionalities, students with disabilities, and/or the gifted.
www.cec.sped.org

COUNCIL FOR LEARNING DISABILITIES
International organization concerned about issues related to students with learning disabilities.
www.cldinternational.org

INDEPENDANT EDUCATIONAL CONSULTANTS ASSOCIATION
The professional association of full-time experienced educational consultants.
www.IECAonline.com

THE INTERNATIONAL DYSLEXIA ASSOCIATION
Dedicated to promoting literacy through research, education, and advocacy.
www.interdys.org/

LEARNING DISABILITIES ASSOCIATION OF AMERTICA
Nonprofit volunteer organization advocating for individuals with learning disabilities.
www.ldanatl.org

NATIONAL CENTER FOR LEARNING DISABILITIES

Ensuring that people with learning disabilities have every opportunity to succeed in school, work and life through programs, advocacy, and research.
www.NCLD.org

SCHWAB LEARNING

A parent's guide to helping kids with learning difficulties.
www.SchwabLearning.org

Source: *K&W Guide to Colleges for Students with Learning Disabilities or Attention Deficit Disorder*, 9th Edition.

BIBLIOGRAPHY

Aspel, Nellie, Jane M. Everson, and David W. Test. *Transition Methods for Youth with Disabilities*. Upper Saddle River, NJ: Pearson Merrill/Prentice Hall, 2006.

Barr, Vickie M., Rhona C. Hartman, and Stephen A. Spillane. "Getting Ready for College: Advising High School Students with Learning Disabilities." *The Postsecondary LD Report*. Ed. Lydia S. Block. Block Educational Consulting, Columbus, OH. Spring 1998. 1–3.

Brinckerhoff, Loring, Joan McGuire, and Stan Shaw. "Differences in High School and College Requirements." *Postsecondary Education and Transition for Students with Learning Disabilities*. Austin, TX: PRO-ED, 2002. 30.

Brinckerhoff, Loring. "High School Students with LD or ADHD: Considering College." SchwabLearning.org. www.schwablearning.org/articles.asp?r=975.

Brinckerhoff, Loring. "Teens with LD and/or AD/HD: Shopping for College Options." SchwabLearning.org. www.schwablearning.org/articles.asp?r=976.

Brinckerhoff, Loring, Joan McGuire, and Stan Shaw. "Timetable for Transitional Planning for Students with Learning Disabilities and ADHD." *Postsecondary Education and Transition for Students with Learning Disabilities*. Austin, TX: PRO-ED, 2002. 38–42.

Brooks, Robert. "How Can Parents Nurture Resilience in Their Children?" SchwabLearning.org. www.schwablearning.org/articles.asp?r=387.

Brown, Dale and Paul Jay Gerber. "Employing People with Learning Disabilities." In Learning Disabilities in Adulthood: Persisting Problems and Evolving Issues. Eds. Paul Jay Gerber and Henry B. Reiff. Austin, TX: PRO-ED, 1995.

Cameto, Renee, Phyllis Levine, and Mary Wagner. Transition Planning for Students with Disabilities. A Special Topic Report of Findings from the National Longitudinal Transition Study-2 (NLTS2). U.S. Department of Education. Menlo Park, CA: SRI International, 2004. www.nlts2.org/reports/2004_11/nlts2_report_2004_11_complete.pdf.

Cameto, Renée, Lynn Newman, and Mary Wagner. National Transition Longitudinal Study-2 (NLTS2). Project Update: Self-Perceptions of Youth with Disabilities: June 14, 2006. U.S. Department of Education. Menlo Park, CA: SRI International, 2006. http://ies.ed.gov/ncser/pdf/NLTS2_Briefing_06_14_06%20.pdf.

The Charles and Helen Schwab Foundation. "Anniversary Survey." Annual unpublished survey given to registered members of SchwabLearning.org. June through December 2005. www.SchwabLearning.org.

The Charles and Helen Schwab Foundation. "How serious a problem is anger management for your child with LD and/or AD/HD?" Online weekly poll conducted during the week of May 23, 2004. SchwabLearning.org. www.schwablearning.org/resources.asp?g=5&s=4&r=156&page=14.

The Charles and Helen Schwab Foundation. "Kids Quiz Charles Schwab About the Personal Side of Learning Disabilities." SchwabLearning.org. www.schwablearning.org/articles.aspx?r=775.

The Charles and Helen Schwab Foundation. "Most Valuable Parent Club Survey." August 3–17, 2006. Online survey given to parents interested in participating in SchwabLearning.org's consumer research (unpublished). August 3–17, 2006. www.SchwabLearning.org.

The Charles and Helen Schwab Foundation. "Would you say that anxiety is a problem for your child with LD and/or AD/HD?" Online weekly poll conducted during the week of June 27, 2004. SchwabLearning.org. www.schwablearning.org/resources.asp?g=5&s=4&r=161& page=13.

Cortellia, Candace. "National Study Follows Youth with Learning Disabilities from High School to Adult Life." Schwab Learning. www.SchwabLearning.org/articles.aspx?r=717.

Dawson, Jodie. "Learning Disabilities and Sibling Issues." SchwabLearning.org. www.schwablearning.org/articles.asp?r=71.

Education Atlas. "The Value of Higher Education." Education Atlas. www.educationatlas.com/value-of-higher-education.html.

Gerber, Paul Jay. "Starting Out Right: Transition to Employment for Young People with LD." Schwab Learning. www.SchwabLearning.org/articles.aspx?r=979.

Gerber, Paul Jay, Rick Ginsberg, and Henry B. Reiff. "Reframing the Learning Disabilities Experience." *Journal of Learning Disabilities* 29, no.1 (1996): 98–101.

Gerber, Paul Jay, Rick Ginsberg, and Henry B. Reiff. "Identifying Alterable Patterns in Employment Success for Highly Successful Adults with Learning Disabilities." *Journal of Learning Disabilities* 25, no.8 (1992): 475–487.

Goldberg, Roberta, Kenneth Herman, Eleanor Higgins, and Marshall Raskind. "Patterns of Change and Predictors of Success in Individuals with Learning Disabilities: Results from a Twenty-year Longitudinal Study." *Learning Disabilities Research and Practice.* 14, no.1 (1999): 35–49.

Kaplan, Jason P. "Sometimes College Should Wait." *Learning Disabilities Journal.* 9, no.2 (1999): 16–19.

Kravets, Marybeth and Imy Wax. *K&W Guide to Colleges for Students with Learning Disabilities.* New York: The Princeton Review, 2007.

Lee, Christopher M. and Rosemary F. Jackson. *Faking It: A Look into the Mind of a Creative Learner.* Portsmouth, NH: Boynton/Cook, 1992.

Levine, Phyllis, Camille Marder, and Mary Wagner. *Services and Supports for Secondary School Students with Disabilities.* A Special Topic Report of Findings from the National Longitudinal Transition Study-2 (NLTS2). Menlo Park, CA: SRI International, 2004. www.nlts2.org/reports/2004_05/nlts2_report_2004_05_co mplete.pdf.

Lyon, G. Reid, Sally E. Shaywitz, and Bennett Shaywitz. "A Definition of Dyslexia" *Annals of Dyslexia.* 53 (2003): 1–14.

Madaus, Joseph W. "Navigating the College Transition Maze: A Guide to Students with Learning Disabilities." *Teaching Exceptional Children.* Jan./Feb. 2005: 32–37.

National Center for Learning Disabilities. "Section 504 Overview." *National Center for Learning Disabilities: The Power to Hope, to Learn, and to Succeed.* www.ncld.org/index.php?option=content&task=view&id=295

National Longitudinal Transition Study-2 (NLTS2). U.S. Department of Education. Menlo Park, CA: SRI International, 2006. http://www.nlts2.org/studymeth/index.html.

National Joint Committee on Learning Disabilities (NJCLD). "Secondary to Postsecondary Education Transition Planning for Students with Learning Disabilities." *Collective Perspectives on Issues Effecting Learning Disabilities: Position Papers and Statements.* Austin: TX: PRO-ED, 1994.165–172.

Norris, Kathleen. "It All Comes Out in the Wash." *New York Times Magazine.* August 22, 1993, Section 6, 16.

Osman, Betty. *Learning Disabilities: A Family Affair.* New York: Warner, 1980.

Osman, Betty. "Learning Disabilities and Sibling Issues." SchwabLearning.org. www.schwablearning.org/articles.asp?r=334.

Osman, Betty. *No One to Play With.* New York: Random House, 1982.

Posthill, Suzanne, and Arlyn Roffman. "The Impact of a Transitional Training Program for Young Adults with Learning Disabilities." *Journal of Learning Disabilities.* 24, no. 10 (1991): 619–29.

Raskind, Marshall. "Expert Answers Guide: Success Attributes of Kids with Learning Disabilities." SchwabLearning.org. www.schwablearning.org/articles.asp?r=876.

Raskind, Marshall. "How Do Kids with LD Become Successful?" SchwabLearning.org. www.schwablearning.org/articles.asp?r=741.

Raskind, Marshall. "Research Trends: Is there a Link between LD and Juvenile Delinquency?" SchwabLearning.org. www.schwablearning.org/articles.asp?r=997.

Raskind, Marshall. "Specific Success Attributes Among Individuals with Learning Disabilities." SchwabLearning.org. www.schwablearning.org/articles.asp?r=742.

Roffman, Arlyn. "LD Talk: Transitioning to Post-School Life." Live online web chat took place on February 28, 2005. Moderated by Dr. Sheldon Horowitz. www.ncld.org/content/view/812/.

Roffman, Arlyn. *Meeting the Challenge of Learning Disabilities in Adulthood.* Baltimore: Brooks, 2000.

Roffman, Arlyn, Jane Herzog, and Pamela Wershba-Gerson. "Helping Young Adults Understand their Learning Disabilities." *Journal of Learning Disabilities.* 27, no. 7 (1994): 413–419.

Rosenfeld, Esq., S. James. "Section 504 and IDEA: Basic Similarities and Differences." Wrightslaw. www.wrightslaw.com/advoc/articles/504_IDEA_Rosenfeld.html.

Sacks, Melinda. "When Your Teenager's Peers Are Headed to College, but He Is Not." SchwabLearning.org. www.schwablearning.org/articles.asp?r=999.

Seligman, Martin. *Helplessness.* San Francisco: W.H. Freeman, 1975.

Shaywitz, Sally E. *Overcoming Dyslexia.* NY: Random House, 2003.

Silver, Larry B. *The Misunderstood Child.* New York: Times Books, 2006.

Smith, Sally. *Succeeding Against the Odds.* Los Angeles: Tarcher, 1991.

Stanberry, Kristin. "Marriage Under Pressure." SchwabLearning.org. www.schwablearning.org/articles.asp?r=316.

Steinle, DeAnn, Mary E. Morningstar, and Sally Smith, eds. *Transition and Your Adolescent with Learning Disabilities; Moving from High School to Postsecondary Education, Training, and Employment.* www.transitioncoalition.org/~tcacs/new/files/adol_convert.pdf.

U.S. Congress. House of Representatives and Senate. Americans with Disabilities Act of 1990. 101th Congress. Jan. 23, 1990. Public Law 101–336. www.usdoj.gov/crt/ada/pubs/ada.txt.

U.S. Congress. House of Representatives and Senate. Individuals with Disabilities Education Improvement Act of 2004 (IDEA). 108th Congress. Dec. 4, 2004. Public Law 108-446. Section 602, 30, A. http://frwebgate.access.gpo.gov/cgi-bin/getdoc.cgi?dbname=108_cong_public_laws&docid=f:publ 446.108.

U.S. Congress. House of Representatives and Senate. Rehabilitation Act of 1973. 93rd Congress. Sept. 42, 1973. Public Law 93–112. www.dotcr.ost.dot.gov/documents/ycr/REHABACT.HTM.

U.S. Department of Education. *Twenty-fifth Annual Report to Congress on the Implementation of the Individuals with Disabilities Education Act 2003.* Students with Disabilities in Postsecondary Education: A Profile of Preparation, Participation, and Outcomes. NCES 1999. www.ed.gov/about/reports/annual/osep/2003/index.html.

Weiss, Lynn. *Give your ADD Teen a Chance.* Colorado Springs: Pinon, 1996.

Wagner, Mary, Lynn Newman, Renée Cameto, Phyllis Levine, and Nicolle Garza. *An Overview of Findings from Wave 2 of the National Longitudinal Transition Study-2 (NLTS2)*. NCSER 2006-3004. U.S. Department of Education. Menlo Park, CA: SRI International, 2006.

NOTES

NOTES

FINDING THE FUNDS:

What you should know about paying for your college education

A year attending a public college on average costs $12,796. Going to a private one will cost you $30,367 per year. Laying down what could be as much as $120,000 if not more over four years is a lot. That's the equivalent of almost 500 iPods, 12,000 movie tickets, or 444,444 packs of instant noodles.

Your parents have a tough job ahead of them. Just about everyone needs some kind of financial assistance. Fortunately, you have many different options, including grants, scholarships, work-study, federal loans, and private loans. Read on to learn about these options and share this with your parents.

OTHER PEOPLE'S MONEY

Scholarships and Grants

These are the best forms of financial aid because they don't have to be paid back. Scholarships are offered to students with unique abilities that the school is seeking to infuse into the student body, such as exceptional talent in music, art, or athletics. However, most scholarships require that you pass and maintain a minimum GPA requirement and some grants may not extend through all four years of your undergraduate education.

Federal grants for undergraduate study include Pell Grants, Federal Supplemental Educational Opportunity Grants (FSEOG), Academic Competitiveness Grants (ACG), and national SMART grants. Pell Grants are the most common type of federal grant awarded to undergraduate students, and form the base upon which supplemental aid from other financing sources may be added. Moreover, Pell Grant recipients receive priority for FSEOG awards, which are provided to students with exceptional financial need, and for National SMART Grants for math and science students.

Academic Competitiveness Grants (ACG) are a brand new kind of grant that began in the 2006–07 academic year. They are for students who have attended secondary school programs that have been qualified by the government as achieving a high standard of academic rigor. As with Federal

Supplemental Educational Opportunity Grants, ACG awards are generally provided as a supplement to students already receiving Federal Pell Grants.

Additionally, your state residency or the state where the school you wish to attend is located also opens you up to state-funded grants and scholarships. Remember to check out the state grant application deadlines found on the FAFSA website mentioned below.

Note that as you advance through your undergraduate education, that progress itself makes you eligible for additional federal, state, and private grant and scholarship opportunities.

Maximize your eligibility for free money by completing the Free Application for Federal Student Aid ("FAFSA") online annually at http://www.fafsa.ed.gov. Visit the Department of Education's student aid portal at http://studentaid.ed.gov for the latest information on federal aid available to students like you. According to the National Center for Education Statistics, approximately 63% of all undergraduates receive some form of financial aid. There is approximately $80 billion in federal grants, loans and work-study funds available out there. Even if you don't think you'll qualify, it is worth it to fill out this form.

Work-study

Federal work-study is another way to lessen the burden of college tuition. Work-study is an actual part-time job, with pay of at least the current federal minimum wage—sometimes higher depending on the type of work you do.

Another advantage of federal work-study is that the program can sometimes place you in jobs related to your field of study. So, while you might be able to get equivalent wages working at a local restaurant or retail store, with work-study, you can sometimes gain resume-building experience related to your degree – in a school laboratory or research center, for example.

How much work-study you receive depends on your level of financial need and the funding level provided by your school. Be aware that work-study alone isn't going to be enough to pay for your education. But, it can be a good way to lessen the sting.

LOANS

When scholarships, grants, and work-study don't cover the full cost of attendance, many students take out loans to help out with the rest.

Avoid loans if you can. A loan can best be described as renting money. There's a cost and it may not be an easy cost to bear.

Here's an interesting anecdote. Many students graduate college without knowing what types of loans they received, who the lender was, and how much they owe. The first time many students become aware of the scope of their obligation is when they receive their first bill—six months after graduation.

This is often because students are passive participants in the financial aid process and do not educate themselves or ask questions. Most students receive a list of "preferred lenders" from their financial aid office and simply go with the lender recommended to them. Over the course of the previous year, relationships between financial aid offices and lenders have been called into question by State Attorneys General, the Department of Education and regulators. Financial aid offices in certain cases received revenue from lenders in exchange for being placed on the "preferred lender list." Some schools have even rented out their name and logo for use on loan applications. These practices occur without disclosure to parents and students.

It is important to know that the "preferred lenders" may not offer the best deals on your loan options. While your financial aid office may be very helpful with scholarships and grants, and is legally required to perform certain duties with regard to federal loans, many do not have staff researching the lowest cost options at the time you are borrowing.

Remember that your tuition payment equals revenue for the school. When borrowing to pay tuition, you can choose to borrow from any lender. That means you can shop for the lowest rate. Keep reading. This will tell you how.

TYPES OF LOANS

The federal government and private commercial lenders offer educational loans to students. Federal loans are usually the "first resort" for borrowers because many are subsidized by the federal government and offer lower interest rates. Private loans have the advantage of fewer restrictions on borrowing limits, but may have higher interest rates and more stringent qualification criteria.

Federal Loans

There are three federal loan programs. The Federal Perkins Loan Program where your school lends you money made available by government funds, the Federal Direct Loan Program (FDLP) where the government lends its money directly to students, and the Federal Family Education Loan Program (FFELP) where financial institutions such as MyRichUncle lend their own money but the government guarantees them. While most schools participate in the Federal Perkins Program, institutions tend to favor either the FFELP or FDLP. You will borrow from FFELP or FDLP depending on which program your school has elected to participate in.

The Federal Perkins Loan is a low-interest (5%) loan for students with exceptional need. Many students who do not qualify or who may need more funds can borrow FFELP or FDLP student loans. Under both programs, the Stafford loan is the typical place to start. The Stafford loan program features a fixed interest rate and yearly caps on the maximum amount a student can borrow. Stafford loans can either be subsidized (the government pays the interest while the student is in school) or unsubsidized (the student is responsible for the interest that accrues while in school). Starting July 1, 2007, the maximum amount an independent freshman student can borrow is $7,500.

It is often assumed that the government sets the rate on student loans. The government does not set the rate of interest. It merely indicates the maximum rate lenders can charge. These lenders are free to charge less than the specified rate of 6.8% for Stafford loans. There is also an origination fee of up to 2% dropping to 1.5% on July 1, 2007. In some cases you may also be charged up to a 1% guarantee fee. Any fees will be taken out of your disbursement.

Historically lenders have hovered at the maximum rate because most loans were distributed via the financial aid office whereby a few lenders received most of the loans. The end result was limited competition. At 1,239 institutions, one lender received more than 90% of the number of Stafford loans in 2006.

Certain lenders offer rate reductions, also known as borrower benefits, conditioned on the borrower making a certain number of on-time payments. Unfortunately, it is estimated that 90% of borrowers never qualify for these reductions.

Last year, MyRichUncle challenged this process by launching a price war. The company cut interest rates on Stafford loans and introduced widespread price competition. These interest rate cuts are effective when students enter repayment and do not have any further qualification requirements. In addition, students only lose the rate reduction if they default.

Parents can also borrow a PLUS loan. The Parent PLUS Loan program allows the parents of dependent students to take out loans to supplement the aid packages of their children. The program allows parents to borrow money to cover any cost not already met by the student's financial aid package up to the full cost of attendance. Unlike the Stafford Loan, eligibility for the Parent PLUS loan is not determined by the FAFSA. A parent fills out a loan application and signs a master promissory note. Eligibility is contingent upon whether the parent has an adverse credit history. Adverse credit history is defined as being no more than 90 days delinquent on any debt, having not declared bankruptcy in the last five years, and having not been the subject of a default determination on a foreclosure, a repossession, a tax lien, a wage garnishment, or a write-off of Title IV debt in the last five years.

The maximum rate a lender can charge for Parent PLUS loans is 8.5%. PLUS loans also have an origination fee of up to 3%, and a guarantee fee of up to 1%. Any fees will be taken out of your disbursement.

Your financial aid office is legally required to certify for lenders that you are enrolled and based on your financial aid package, the amount in Federal loans

Let's say you have no credit history or a credit-worthy co-borrower You might consider PrePrime™: a new underwriting methodology pioneered by MyRichUncle. Instead of focusing solely on credit history and co-borrowers, MyRichUncle with its PrePrime™ option also takes into account academic performance, student behavior, and other factors that can indicate that a student will be a responsible borrower. The success of the PrePrime™ model has proven that good students make good borrowers. And it makes MyRichUncle the first true provider of student loans.

you are eligible to borrow. You are free to choose any lender even if the lender is not on your financial aid office's preferred lender list.

To shop for low cost Federal loans, call a number of lenders before applying to determine their rates and fees. This is an effective approach because your application will not impact the price. Once you are comfortable that you have the lowest cost option, apply and submit the Master Promissory Note to your lender of choice.

Private Loans

Private student loans can make it possible to cover the costs of higher education when other sources of funding have been exhausted. Additionally, when you apply for federal loans, you can borrow up to what your institution has pre-defined as the annual cost of attendance. If your anticipated expenses are above and beyond this pre-defined cost because of your unique needs, it will take a series of appeals before your institution will allow you to borrow more federal loans. Private loans help you meet your true expectation of what you will need financially. Private loans can pay expenses that federal loans can't, such as application and testing fees and the cost of transportation.

When you apply for a private loan, the lending institution will check your credit history including your credit score and determine your capacity to pay back the money you borrow. For individuals whose credit history is less than positive, lenders may require a co-borrower: a credit-worthy individual who also agrees to be accountable to the terms of the loan. While private loans do not have annual borrowing limits, they often have higher interest rates, and interest rate caps are higher than those set by Federal loans. Generally, the loans are variable rate loans so the interest rate may go up or down, changing the cost.

To shop for a private loan, after you've researched several options, apply to as many of them as you feel comfortable. Once you are approved, compare rates. Pick the lowest cost option.

EXTRA LESSONS

Borrow the minimum

Just because someone is offering to lend you thousands upon thousands of dollars doesn't mean you should necessarily take them up on that offer. At some point, you'll have to repay the debt and you'll have to do it responsibly. Wouldn't it be better to use your money for something more worthwhile to you?

Know your rights

Currently, student lending is an industry that is under heavy scrutiny. It is important, now more than ever, for parents and students to have an active voice and to make educational and financial choices that are right for them. Some schools work with "preferred lenders" when offering federal and private loans. You are not required to choose a loan from one of these lenders if you can find a better offer. With respect to federal loans the financial aid office has a legislated role which is to certify for the lending institution that you the borrower are indeed enrolled and the amount you are eligible for. They are not legally empowered to dictate your choice of lender and must certify your loan from the lender of your choice. You have the right to shop for and to secure the best rates possible for your loans. Don't get bullied into choosing a different lender, simply because it is preferred by an institution. Instead, do your homework and make sure you understand all of your options.

Know what you want

When it's all said and done, you will have to take a variety of factors into account in order to choose the best school for you and for your future. You shouldn't have to mortgage your future to follow a dream, but you also shouldn't downgrade this opportunity just to save a few bucks.

An out-of-the-box approach

Community colleges are a viable option for those ultimately seeking a four-year degree. Articulation agreements between community colleges and major four-year institutions allow students to complete their general education requirements at community colleges and have them transferred to a four-year institution. If you are really keen on graduating from that fancy four year college of your choice, transferring in from a community college is a cheaper path to getting that same degree. At an average cost of $2,272 per year, it is a thought worth exploring.

MYRICHUNCLE

Who we are:

MyRichUncle is a national student loan company offering federal (Stafford, PLUS and GradPLUS) and private loans to undergraduate, graduate, and professional students. MyRichUncle knows that getting a student loan can be a complicated and intimidating process, so we changed it. We believe students are credit-worthy borrowers, and that student loan debt should be taken seriously by borrowers and lenders alike. We propose changes in the student loan industry that will better serve parents, schools, and most importantly, students.

Why it matters:

Your student loan will be your responsibility. When you enter into a loan agreement, you're entering into a long-term relationship with your lender—15 years, on average. The right student loan with the right lender can help you avoid years of unnecessary fees and payments.

What we do:

MyRichUncle pays close attention to the obstacles students face. Removing these obstacles drives everything we do. MyRichUncle discounts federal loan rates at repayment rather than requiring years of continuous payments to earn the discount, which saves you money right from the start. We help you plan ahead, so you can choose the best loans and save.

Our credentials:

MyRichUncle is a NASDAQ listed company. Our symbol is UNCL. In 2006, MyRichUncle was featured in FastCompany Magazine's Fast 50 and in Businessweek's Top Tech Entrepreneurs. MyRichUncle and its parent company, MRU Holdings, are financed by a number of leading investment banks and venture capitalists, including subsidiaries of Merrill Lynch, Lehman Brothers, Battery Ventures and Nomura Holdings.

Call us:
1-800-926-5320

or learn more online:
MYRICHUNCLE.COM/TLD

MYRICHUNCLE
STUDENT LOANS

More expert advice from The Princeton Review

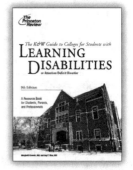

Life after High School:
Action Tips for
Parents and Teens

SchwabLearning.org

A Parent's Guide to Helping Kids with Learning Difficulties

Schwab Learning

Helping kids with learning and attention problems be successful in school and life

Dear Parent:

When our son was in the second grade, he struggled to read, and he was ultimately identified with dyslexia. At the time, it was difficult for me and my wife, Helen, to find reliable information that could help us understand his learning disability. We established Schwab Learning, a nonprofit program of the Charles and Helen Schwab Foundation, to help other parents who were experiencing the same frustrations.

Kids who struggle in school need to know that it is okay to learn differently, that everyone has their own strengths and challenges, and that their talents can help them achieve their dreams.

Children with learning difficulties can learn. Kids who struggle in the classroom *can* succeed in school and life. By providing information, guidance, and encouragement to parents, teachers, and children, Schwab Learning helps families and teachers work together to positively affect the lives of kids with learning difficulties. You can learn more about our resources in the following pages.

Sincerely,

Charles Schwab

Introduction

Learning to live independently is challenging for all young people making the transition to adulthood. *But it can be especially daunting for those with learning and attention problems — and their parents.* For that reason, developing clear transition goals and plans can be one of the most important efforts you and your teenager undertake together.

To pave the way for your teen's transition to adulthood, you'll want to:

➤ Start the transition process early.

➤ Encourage your teenager to participate in the transition process, and to eventually manage it himself.

➤ Adopt an attitude of high expectations, balanced with openness and flexibility, about your child's goals and strategies.

➤ Help your teen learn his rights under federal law and how to advocate for himself.

Indeed, this is a tall order for you and your teenager. To help you through the transition process, Schwab Learning has developed several action-oriented tips that address specific aspects of transition. Some of the tips are aimed at you, the parent, while other suggestions speak directly to your teenager.

We wish you and your teenager a successful and satisfying journey.

IDEA 2004: Transition Planning for Life after High School

If your high school student has an Individualized Education Program (IEP), she's entitled to transition services from her public school by federal law. Transition services include helping her make plans for a job, school, or training after high school. Parents must play a key role in this process.

The Individuals with Disabilities Education Act (IDEA) requires that a school's transition services "promote a successful transition from high school to postsecondary education or employment, and independent living."

You are a full and equal member of the IEP team, so when the team meets to discuss transition needs, make sure your child's plan meets the following requirements.

Your teen's IEP team must:

➤ **Develop appropriate, measurable postsecondary goals**, based upon age-appropriate transition assessments related to training, education, employment, and, where appropriate, independent living skills.

- These goals should reflect your teen's strengths, preferences, and interests.
- Age-appropriate transition assessments might include such things as interest inventories and other assessment tools to help identify an individual's special talents.

➤ **Develop a statement that describes the transition services** (including courses of study) needed to assist the student in reaching those goals.

➤ **Provide a "Summary of Performance"** to students whose special education eligibility is terminating due to graduation or age. This new summary must include information on the student's academic achievement and functional performance and include recommendations on how to assist the student in meeting postsecondary goals.

Adapted from SchwabLearning.org's article, "IDEA 2004 Close Up: Transition Planning," by Candace Cortiella. *Read this full article at*: **http://www.schwablearning.org/idea2004**

Tech Prep and Assistive Technology

Colleges and employers rely increasingly on the use of technology. Today's teens — especially those with learning disabilities (LD) — may benefit from using technology in school, at home, on the job, and in social settings. The IEP for a college-bound teen should include objectives for both mainstream educational technologies (e.g., laptop computer) and assistive technology.

Mainstream Technologies

Consider your teen's tech readiness for college by helping him evaluate his current technical skills. Next, you'll want to help him identify additional technology skills he plans to develop before college, and learn about the technology skill requirements and support at the colleges he is considering. To begin this process, download the worksheet on SchwabLearning.org:

"Questions to Help Teens Assess Their Tech Readiness for College" at **http://www.schwablearning.org/tech_assess**

Assistive Technology

Assistive technology (AT) for kids with LD is defined as any device, piece of equipment, or system that helps bypass, work around, or compensate for an individual's specific learning deficits. Review which tools your teen is using now, and consider what might be helpful in college or the workplace. For example:

Area of Learning Difficulty	Some Helpful AT Tools
Reading	Audio Books Speech Synthesizer/Screen Reader Variable Speed Tape Recorder
Writing	Graphic Organizer Portable Word Processor Talking Spell-checker
Math	Electronic Math Worksheet Talking Calculator
Memory and Organization	Free-form Database Software Information/Data Manager
Listening	Personal FM Listening System Variable Speed Tape Recorder

Suggested Resources:

"E-ssential Guide: A Parent's Guide to Assistive Technology"
http://www.schwablearning.org/atguide

Schwab Learning's interactive Assistive Technology database
http://www.schwablearning.org/attools

. . . .

Helping Your Teen Develop Daily Living Skills

All young people must develop a number of daily living skills before they
can live successfully on their own.

Daily living skills fall into six areas:

- ➤ meal preparation
- ➤ money management
- ➤ housekeeping
- ➤ self-care (e.g., hygiene, medical care)
- ➤ planning leisure time and activities
- ➤ getting around (e.g., transportation)

According to Arlyn Roffman, Ph.D., research shows that many teens and
young adults with LD find it difficult to acquire these skills.

How can you, as a parent, help your child develop daily living skills?

- ➤ **Determine how your child's LD creates challenges to
  mastering certain skills.** *For example:* A teen who struggles
  with reading may need help deciphering washing instructions
  on a piece of clothing.
- ➤ **Provide clear and explicit instruction when teaching daily
  living skills.** *For example:* While shopping for groceries, talk
  your teen through the process of calculating the sale price of
  a product.

➤ **Encourage hands-on training, and remember that practice is the key.** *For example:* Have your teen place her allowance, earnings, and other cash in an envelope and budget her expenditures each month.

➤ **Resist the temptation to perform daily living tasks for your teen.** *For example:* Allow him to practice and master each skill without your help. Have him sort, wash, press, and fold his own clothes.

➤ **Build on your child's strengths.** *For example:* If your child has a "green thumb" have him take responsibility for watering and fertilizing the plants in your home.

Adapted from SchwabLearning.org's article, "Toward Independence: Helping Teens Prepare For Life on Their Own," by Arlyn Roffman, Ph.D. *Read this full article at*: **http://www. schwablearning.org/independence**

Worksheet for Evaluating Daily Living Skills

It can be daunting to think about teaching your teen with LD the many skills required to live on his own. It may be just as overwhelming for him to learn them! This worksheet is designed to help you and your teen create a plan for him to develop household skills.

Ask your teen the following questions and complete this form together.

➤ What kinds of learning disabilities do you struggle with the most?

➤ What daily living skills might be difficult to learn because of them?

➤ What accommodations help you deal with your learning disabilities in school? How could you adapt those accommodations to learn daily living skills?

➤ When you think about going to college and/or living on your own, what daily living skills do you worry about most?

➤ How might you plan to learn and practice the daily skills that you don't feel proficient in?

➤ As you learn certain daily living skills, create a list of those you've mastered.

Helping Your Teen Find a Part-Time Job

For kids who struggle in school, a job outside of school can offer a practical, concrete way for them to feel successful, and to receive tangible rewards.

Quick tips for a successful job search:

➤ Start Small

- Help your teen set realistic job expectations—an entry-level position, rather than his fantasy job.

➤ Volunteer to Gain Work Experience

- Volunteering is often the best way for kids to enter the work force and gain work experience.

➤ Who Do You Know?

- Call in favors with employers you know and consider going in with your teen to provide an introduction.

➤ Finding the Right Job

- Help your teen identify his strengths and interests so he'll know which types of jobs to apply for. And, have him talk with school counselors and teachers for job suggestions.

➤ What to Wear, What to Say

- Talk about appropriate attire for different types of jobs.
- The job interview can be challenging and scary. Role playing and written notes can help.

➤ Review the Paperwork

- Have your teen complete the application in pencil first, and review it together before handing it in to a potential employer.

➤ Persistence Pays

- Encourage your child to check back with the employer about the status of his application, rather than waiting to hear from them.

Adapted from SchwabLearning.org's article, "Teens with LD: Finding a Summer Job," by Melinda Sacks. *Read this full article at*: **http://www.schwablearning.org/job**

Questions to Ask If Your Teen with Learning Disabilities Is Considering College

Today's teenagers have a wide array of college options from which to choose, so it's helpful for teens and their parents to have guidelines to inform their decision. And, of course, kids with LD have additional needs and considerations.

Discuss these questions with your teenager:

➤ Is your teenager fully aware of how his LD affects him academically, socially, and in other ways?

➤ Is your teenager self-confident and aware of his strengths and talents? How does he demonstrate this in his school work and life choices?

➤ Is he able to advocate for the accommodations he needs to succeed? For example, is he an active participant in his IEP meetings?

➤ Would your teenager rather: (check the appropriate box)

    ☐ attend college full-time

    ☐ attend college part-time while working part-time

    ☐ work full-time for awhile before deciding whether to attend college

➤ Does he understand how college differs from high school? For example, in college, students spend less time in class and more time studying independently. It's also important to know that securing any necessary accommodations is the responsibility of the student, not the college.

➤ Of the following college options, which holds the greatest appeal for your teenager? (check the appropriate box)

    ☐ A four-year college away from home

    ☐ A four-year college near home

    ☐ Community college

    ☐ Vocational education or trade school

    ☐ Online learning or distance learning

    ☐ Other: _____

➤ Do you think your teen would be willing to seek support from a campus disability services office, if needed?

➤ What does your teenager hope to accomplish by attending college? (Check all that apply)

☐ To major in a program area he feels passionate about

☐ To earn a degree or certificate that will help him get a good job

☐ To take a few classes in subjects that interest him, without necessarily earning a degree

☐ To participate in college life and campus activities

☐ To get a "fresh start" in a place where no one knows him

☐ Other _____

➤ Would your teen be comfortable living away from home while attending college? If so, is he ready to consider the pros and cons of dorm life versus living in an apartment with roommates?

Remember that your teen's preferences and goals may change over time, so work together to update this questionnaire periodically.

Suggested Resources:

"Expert Answers Guide: College for Students with LD and AD/HD," by Loring Brinckerhoff, Ph.D. **http://www.schwablearning.org/ expertanswers/brinck**

"Attorney Paul Grossman on Legal Rights for College Students with LD" **http://www.schwablearning.org/grossman**

When Your Teen's Peers Are Headed to College—and He's Not

College may not be the best option for every teenager. That doesn't mean your teen has to feel left out while his peers are visiting colleges. You and your teen can still explore alternative programs that will help to prepare him for successful employment after high school.

Here's how to start:

➤ Sit down with your teen and make a list of his interests, skills, and talents.

➤ Based on that list, start looking at positive, realistic post-high school opportunities.

➤ Consider a summer job that could provide your teen with "real world" experience in his field of interest.

➤ Develop a list of programs or training centers your teen would like to visit.

➤ Schedule your visits to these places to coincide with peers' college visits.

This carefully considered "action plan" will also help your teen respond to well-meaning family or friends who ask, "So where do you want to go to college?"

Here are some other ways your child can answer the "college" question:

➤ I'm taking some time off after high school to consider alternatives.

➤ I'm going to work for awhile and save up some money.

➤ I'm going to take classes at the local junior college.

Your patience and flexibility in this process will reap big benefits for your teen's confidence—and competence.

Adapted from SchwabLearning.org's article "When Your Teenager's Peers Are Headed to College, but He Is Not," by Melinda Sacks. *Read this full article at:* **http://www.schwablearning.org/collegealts**

What Will I Gain or Lose by Telling My Boss (or Others) about My Learning Disability?

It may feel risky to tell someone at work, school, or in your social circle that you have an LD. While there could be benefits to disclosing your LD, there could also be costs. So, how do you decide?

Write down your answers to the following questions to help you think through your decision to disclose your LD.

➤ What could I potentially gain by disclosing my LD? *For example:*

- Would it open the door to accommodations that would help me be more productive?

- Would it help me build closer relationships because I trusted friends with knowing about my LD?

➤ What could I potentially lose? *For example:*

- Would the person equate LD with a lack of intelligence and assume I wasn't competent?

- Would my boss think it was going to require a lot of extra time and money to "work around" my LD?

➤ Could I live with the potential losses of disclosing my LD? *For example:*

- Could I accept never getting promoted to a supervisory position, due to my boss not understanding the LD?

- Could I live with losing this person's respect or friendship if they thought less of me just because of my LD?

➤ Do the potential gains of self-disclosure outweigh the "acceptable" losses? *For example:*

- I really want to get promoted. I would need additional training, which would be challenging because of my reading disability. Can I risk having my boss think I'm not competent by asking for reading software?

Each decision you make about disclosing your LD will be different. Get input from family, friends, or colleagues. Then you can act with confidence.

Adapted from SchwabLearning.org's article, "Self-disclosure of Learning Disabilities in the Beyond-School Years," by Paul Gerber, Ph.D. *Read this full article at:* **http://www. schwablearning.org/disclosure**

. . . .

A Winning Plan to Prepare for College

Congratulations on making the decision to apply for college! Having an LD poses some extra challenges, but the following tips will help you move forward with your college plans.

➤ **Take the lead.** Be proactive in working with your IEP team and designing your transition plan.

➤ **Keep your strengths, talents, and interests in mind** — not just your learning challenges — when considering colleges.

➤ **Be clear about the accommodations you will need to succeed.** Collect documentation (proof) that you need certain accommodations.

➤ **Learn to advocate for yourself — and your needs — now.** Practice this skill in high school so you'll be comfortable doing so in college.

Jonathan Mooney, a public speaker and successful young adult with LD, offers great advice for students with LD who are researching colleges and universities:

1. First, search for schools that have the right "vibe" and academic programs you feel passionate about.

2. Next, look at that list of schools and determine which of them have well-run, accessible learning programs.

3. Look for schools that welcome students of various ethnicities, cultures, and disabilities.

4. Find out what the curriculum requirements are at each school. Some may be too strict or rigid for you.

5. Go beyond the (campus) learning support center to find out if the college will really support your needs. Do this by talking to faculty in the departments you're interested in. Talk to other students, too.

Adapted from SchwabLearning.org's interview, "Jonathan Mooney on Goal Setting and Motivation." *Read this full article at:* **http://www.schwablearning.org/mooney**

Online Resources

SchwabLearning.org

www.SchwabLearning.org is a parent's guide to helping kids with learning difficulties. We'll help you understand how to:

- **Identify** your child's problem by working with teachers, doctors, and other professionals.

- **Manage** your child's challenges at school and home by collaborating with teachers to obtain educational and behavioral support, and by using effective parenting strategies.

- **Connect** with other parents who know what you are going through. You'll find support and inspiration in their personal stories and on our Parent-to-Parent Message Board.

- **Locate resources,** including Schwab Learning publications, plus additional book: and websites.

SchwabLearning.org — free and reliable information at your fingertips, 24 hours day, seven days a week.

SparkTop.org™

www.SparkTop.org is a one-of-a-kind website created expressly for kid: ages 8-12 with learning difficulties, including learning disabilities (LD) and Attention-Deficit/Hyperactivity Disorder (AD/HD). Through games, activities and creativity tools, kids at SparkTop.org can:

- Get tips on how to succeed in school and life.

- Showcase their creativity and be recognized for their strengths.

- Safely connect with other kids who know what they are going through.

SparkTop.org is free, carries no advertising, and is fully compliant with the Children's Online Privacy Protection Act (COPPA).